WHAT ABOUT ME?

WHAT ABOUT ME?

GET OUT OF YOUR OWN WAY AND DISCOVER THE POWER OF AN UNSELFISH LIFE

JOYCE MEYER

NEW YORK · NASHVILLE

FaithWords
Hachette Book Group
1290 Avenue of the Americas, New York, NY 10104
faithwords.com
twitter.com/faithwords

First Edition: September 2024

FaithWords is a division of Hachette Book Group, Inc. The FaithWords name and logo are registered trademarks of Hachette Book Group, Inc.

The publisher is not responsible for websites (or their content) that are not owned by the publisher.

The Hachette Speakers Bureau provides a wide range of authors for speaking events. To find out more, go to hachettespeakersbureau.com or email HachetteSpeakers@hbgusa.com.

FaithWords books may be purchased in bulk for business, educational, or promotional use. For information, please contact your local bookseller or the Hachette Book Group Special Markets Department at special.markets@hbgusa.com.

Library of Congress Cataloging-in-Publication Data has been applied for.

ISBNs: 978-1-5460-4698-1 (hardcover), 978-1-5460-0489-9 (large type), 978-1-5460-4700-1 (ebook)

Printed in the United States of America

LSC-C

Printing 2, 2024

CONTENTS

INTRODUCTION

And He died for all, so that all those who live might live no longer to and for themselves, but to and for Him Who died and was raised again for their sake.

2 Corinthians 5:15

I titled this book *What About Me?* because of something God spoke to my heart many years ago. I had been a Christian for a long time but had not grown much spiritually, so in terms of my spiritual development, I was still a baby Christian. I remained selfish and self-centered. My life revolved around what I wanted, what I thought, and how I felt. In addition, I was filled with self-pity. Every morning, I woke up thinking about myself, and I was foremost in my mind throughout each day.

One morning while lying in bed, immediately after waking up, I started thinking about myself, what I planned to do that day, and what my family would do. Dave was headed to play golf, and the kids were going swimming in the neighborhood pool. I thought, *Everyone else is going to have fun, and I guess I will just work all day.* My mood sank, and I thought, *What about me?!*

Suddenly, the Holy Spirit began to whisper in my heart and show me a picture of what I was like. I envisioned the devil putting this thought in my head repeatedly: *What about me? What about me? What about me?* God showed me that I reminded Him of a little robot the devil wound up every morning with selfish thoughts, and all He heard out of me all day long was "What about me?" "What about me?" "What about me? *Beep. Beep.* What about me?" He revealed to me in just a few seconds just how selfish I was. Simply acknowledging this reality was painful. *Very* painful.

I began to share this story in my teachings, pretending to be the "What about me?" robot. Everyone seemed to relate, and soon the little robot became famous. I've used this example in many countries overseas, as well as in the United States, and no matter what language people speak, they seem to relate to the selfish little robot that only says "What about me?" all day long.

It was difficult for me to admit that I was selfish, and I think it's hard for all of us. But facing my self-centeredness and letting God deal with it was life-changing for me, and I believe it will be for you too. Learning to live an unselfish life may seem to be an unlikely path to happiness and blessing, but I promise you: It is.

Jesus died for us to be set free from sin and its consequences and from other forms of bondage, one of which is selfishness. Perhaps you have never considered selfishness as a type of bondage. I hadn't until about thirty years ago when I was praying and asking God why I was so unhappy. I had a very nice life and no reason to be unhappy, yet I was. God immediately spoke to my heart and showed me that I was unhappy because I was selfish. If you know how much God loves you, it will not bother you when He shows you something about yourself that needs to be corrected. You can rejoice when He corrects you because you know everything He does in your life is for your benefit. He corrects us only in order to help us change for the better so we can enjoy our lives more.

I was unhappy because I was selfish.

The knowledge that I was selfish opened a whole new avenue

of study in God's Word for me, and I found that His Word backs up what I believed I had heard from Him about selfishness in my life. Second Corinthians 5:15, the scripture on which this book is based, says plainly that one reason Jesus died for us was so we might no longer live only for ourselves but for Him. We belong to God. We have been purchased with the blood of Jesus (1 Corinthians 6:20; 1 Peter 1:18–19). We were bought with a price; therefore, we are no longer our own. We live for the Lord (Romans 14:8).

> Do you not know that your body is the temple (the very sanctuary) of the Holy Spirit Who lives within you, Whom you have received [as a Gift] from God? You are not your own, you were bought with a price [purchased with a preciousness and paid for, made His own]. So then, honor God and bring glory to Him in your body.
>
> 1 Corinthians 6:19–20

A friend recently said to me, "People are excited about the fact that the blood of Jesus was shed for the remission of their sins, but they forget that it also bought them and they are no longer their own."

A simple definition of spiritual maturity is "dying to self and living for Jesus." When we become givers instead of takers, we become more like God, because He is a giver. He gives and gives and keeps on giving. He gave us Jesus, and He has forgiven our sin. He gives mercy, grace, help, strength, joy, righteousness, wisdom, knowledge, creative ideas, and so many more blessings that I

When you become a giver instead of a taker, you become more like God.

would run out of room if I tried to list them all. He gives to those who are deserving and those who are not. Ask yourself: "What has God ever done but give to me?" He never takes anything but your love, praise, worship, and thanksgiving.

God wants us to obey Him because we love Him and because obedience to Him is the pathway to happiness and the enjoyment of our life. He wants us to have the desires of our hearts and to prosper and succeed (Psalm 37:4, 1:3).

John 10:10 tells us that Jesus came that we might have and enjoy our lives abundantly. If we are willing to obey Him, we will have an abundance of joy and enjoyment in our lives. One way to obey Him is to be unselfish and willing to sacrifice for others. Are you ready to be a giver instead of a taker? I'm not talking about merely giving financially, but giving in all areas of life. Live to give instead of living to get.

God did not send His Son to redeem us so we could live selfishly, spending our lives trying to get what we want, but so we can allow Him to work through us to help other people. We are Christ's ambassadors on earth, and He makes His appeal to people through us (2 Corinthians 5:20). If we will do as He asks of us, He will take care of us and give us much more than we could ever manage to get for ourselves. Don't miss this point: *If we will do as He asks of us, He will take care of us and give us much more than we could ever manage to get for ourselves.* It will also lead to greater happiness than we have ever imagined. If you remember this truth as you read this book, doing what God wants you to do will be much easier than it will be if you don't. God is the Rewarder of those who diligently seek Him (Hebrews 11:6). He always rewards obedience and faithfulness.

Living selfishly is like living in solitary confinement. Generally speaking, no one means more to us than we mean to ourselves, and when we allow ourselves to live with ourselves as our main focus and top priority, we find ourselves lonely and unfulfilled. We want to be happy, but we get in our own way when we are self-centered. We are not created to live selfishly, but to reach out to others. And as we do, we will experience a life worth living.

We are born selfish and stingy, but when we accept Jesus as our Savior we are born *again* unselfish and generous. We simply need to learn to walk in our new nature, and that's what this book is about. From this point forward, don't think of yourself as selfish. Think as the new creation God has made you to be in Christ (2 Corinthians 5:17), and agree with God that you are generous because His nature lives in you. Spend time each day intentionally thinking about what you can do for others.

The apostle Paul teaches us to walk in the Spirit so we will not fulfill the cravings and desires of the flesh (Galatians 5:16). This means the only way to live a truly unselfish life is to live a Spirit-filled life, relying on the Spirit's power and grace in every situation. I have devoted two chapters in this book to the importance of walking in the Spirit, so here I will simply say that I don't believe we can live as unselfish people without the Holy Spirit's help. Thankfully, according to John 14:26 (NKJV), the Holy Spirit is our Helper, and He is always available to help us live as God calls us to live.

The first step toward an unselfish life is to *desire* to live unselfishly. Once we have the desire, we learn how to be unselfish through studying God's Word and through prayer and practicing unselfish living. We need an understanding of our human nature, and we need to understand that there is a difference between what we want, what we think, what we feel, and God's will.

"What about me?" runs through our minds frequently. We tend to ask, sometimes subconsciously, *What am I going to get out of this?* before we make certain decisions or take certain actions, especially those that are hard to take. But if we will accept the challenge to live unselfishly, we can learn to live as Jesus did and share His joy.

In the world, when someone asks you to do something, and you inquire, "What am I going to get out of this?" you cannot always trust their answer. People may not keep their promises to you, but when God promises to do something, He never fails to do it. God is faithful and He cannot lie (Numbers 23:19; Psalm 31:3–5).

I pray you truly desire to be like Jesus and learn to think of others more than you think about yourself, trusting Him to take care of you. And I pray that you will be willing to do hard things now for the joy you will receive later. This book is about learning to love and the joy it brings. And I believe that if you will follow the principles you learn from it, you will finally find the joy and fulfillment you are searching for.

> *Be willing to do hard things now for the joy you will receive later.*

PART 1

Learning to Love

CHAPTER 1
I Was Always on My Mind

Treat others the same way you want them to treat you.

Luke 6:31 AMP

I've met many people who seem to live with a vague sense of unhappiness and seem to be constantly in search of something that will give them the joy and peace they crave. Maybe you can relate to this because you, too, find yourself going through the motions of life, fulfilling your responsibilities, but thinking *I'm just not happy.* Other people may see you as capable, smart, and dependable—and maybe you receive lots of applause and affirmation for your abilities—but deep inside, you feel unfulfilled and lack the sense of satisfaction and contentment you long for. Perhaps nothing is terribly wrong in your life. You aren't going through a major crisis, and you haven't suffered a significant loss. But still, inside of you, there's a place of emptiness. Something is missing.

When we feel that vague sense of unhappiness I mentioned, human nature is to look around us to figure out what's wrong. We say to ourselves:

- "If I had a better boss, I would be happy."
- "If my kids would just behave, I would be happy."
- "If I could move out of this noisy apartment and buy a house, I would be happy."
- "If my husband would help around the house, I would be happy."
- "If I didn't have so much stress at work, I would be happy."
- "If I could lose weight, I would be happy."
- "If my parents had treated me better when I was growing up, I would be happy."
- "If I could find a way to pursue my dream, I would be happy."
- "If I could finish school, I would be happy."
- "If I could get out of debt, I would be happy."

We typically look to our circumstances to identify what needs to change in order to make us happy. I know this because I did it for many years. I finally discovered that the problem was not in some situation *around* me; it was *within* me. I sum it up like this: I was always on my mind.

For the first twenty years of my Christian life, I have to admit that most of my thinking was self-centered. I learned to think this way as a child. Like many people, I grew up in a dysfunctional home, and I was sexually abused by my father. My mother, though physically present in my life, abandoned me to the abuse by not dealing with it and not getting me the help I needed. It's an understatement to say that I was deeply disappointed in my relationship with my parents. I was also disappointed in other relationships, so I made the decision—actually a vow—early in life that I would not depend on anyone for anything. I would take care of myself.

As years went by and I became an adult, I didn't know how to change my self-focused thinking—or even that it needed to change. I knew I wasn't happy, but I had no idea that the root of my discontentment was in my selfish thinking and behavior. I tried to arrange everything in such a way that I got what I wanted. I planned the meals for our family, and on the rare occasions when we went out to eat, I chose the restaurant. In those days, we had only one television set, and when we watched television, I became angry if I didn't get to watch what I wanted to watch. On Sundays after we returned home from church, Dave almost always watched sports, and I spent the day feeling sorry for myself because I had worked all week. Since I didn't like sports, nothing he wanted to watch interested me. Considering my actions after church, it's obvious that going to a worship service did not affect my behavior.

If Dave played golf on Saturdays, which he usually did, I also got angry because I wanted him to stay home and do something with me. I thought it was not fair for him to enjoy himself, and

I thought his pursuit of the activities he enjoyed left me with nothing to do but work around the house. Of course, working was my choice, and often, while Dave watched athletic events, I chose to clean and make a lot of noise doing it, hoping to make him feel guilty for just sitting and enjoying himself. But it never worked. I could have chosen many other things to do, but since I didn't get my way, I was determined to pout and feel sorry for myself.

During those years, everything was about me, me, me! I didn't stop to consider that Dave went to work every day, and although I worked hard as a stay-at-home mom, I also had time to do things I wanted to do. I went shopping with friends, took my children swimming, and did other activities, but I begrudged Dave watching a football game. I could have chosen to sit with him and let him teach me about the game, but I wasn't even willing to try to learn because of my ridiculous anger and selfishness. I needed to learn to love him enough to want him to enjoy himself even if it meant sacrifice for me. Real love sacrifices for the ones it loves.

During those years, I was like Martha in the Bible, who became angry with her sister Mary. Martha was upset because she was doing all the work involved in hosting Jesus in their home, while Mary sat at Jesus' feet and listened to Him teach (Luke 10:38–42). Jesus told Martha she was anxious and worried about many things, but that Mary had chosen the better thing (Luke 10:41–42), which was to be in His presence and learn from Him. I pray that you and I will continually and increasingly be like Mary, choosing not to be anxious or worried, but living in peace and enjoying God's presence. One key to doing this is getting our focus off ourselves.

Now be honest with yourself: As you read about my past behavior, does any of it seem like yours? If not, you are blessed, but if so, this book is an opportunity to recognize it and begin to make some changes that will lead to great blessings in your life.

I can truly say that for years I was always on my mind. I am so grateful to God for changing me and setting me free from being selfish and self-centered. I would not say I am totally free, because I still see selfishness creeping into my life regularly, but at least I have made progress, and I now know that being selfish is not the pathway to joy. I think selfishness is something we will always be tempted with and need to resist, so don't feel bad if it rears its ugly head in your life too from time to time.

I try to keep in mind what Jesus says in Matthew 10:39: "Whoever finds his [lower] life will lose it [the higher life], and whoever loses his [lower] life on My account will find it [the higher life]." He is saying that if we choose to unselfishly lose our lower life in this world, we will find the higher life, which is far better. As you continue in this book, may you be encouraged to let go of the lower life (selfishness) and experience the higher life (unselfishness) God wants you to live.

Loving people not only makes them happy; it makes us happy too. But selfishness steals our joy. When we are selfish, we may think we are getting what we want, but the truth is that

> *Selfishness steals your joy.*

it still won't make us happy because selfishness isn't God's will.

There are, of course, times to stand up for yourself, and you do deserve some of the things you want in life, but the best way to get them is to let God give them to you while you choose to behave as Jesus would in every situation.

The Importance of Living Unselfishly

If I had to summarize in one sentence why living unselfishly is important, I would say this: Unselfish living is God's will, and it makes us happy! One of the points I have emphasized for years in my teachings is that God wants us to *enjoy* our lives. Jesus was a joyful person, and He wants us to be joyful too. In John 15:11, Jesus has been giving His disciples many important instructions and says to them: "I have told you these things, *that My joy and delight may be in you, and that your joy and gladness may be of full measure and complete and overflowing*" (emphasis mine).

Interestingly, the next comment Jesus makes after talking about joy is about unselfish living: "This is My commandment: that you love one another [just] as I have loved you. No one has greater love [no one has shown stronger affection] than to lay down (give up) his own life for his friends" (John 15:12–13). We can see clearly that the path to joy is to live focused on others, not on ourselves. When you initially begin to live the unselfish life, it will be difficult. But the longer you do it, the more joy you will find as a result.

The apostle Paul writes in Philippians 4:5, "Let all men know and perceive and recognize your unselfishness (your considerateness, your forbearing spirit). The Lord is near [He is coming soon]." This teaches us that our Lord wants us to live unselfishly and He wants the world to recognize it as an example of the way He loves everyone. Unselfish living is even more important as Christ's return draws near. Time is short, and we want to live in ways that will cause people to want a relationship with Jesus before it's too late. The way to do this is to show them genuine unconditional love. We are not only to love people who are easy to love, but also to love those who are difficult to love. If you would like help in this area, consider reading my book *Loving People Who Are Hard to Love*.

The world is filled with darkness, but Jesus says that, as believers, we are the light of the world, and we should let our light shine (Matthew 5:16). He also says that we are the salt of the earth, and we must remain salty (Matthew 5:13) because salt gives food flavor. Without salt, food is bland and tasteless. Christians are the flavor in the world. Just imagine what the world would be like if the Holy Spirit were not present and active in our world, and if there were no Christians. It would be filled with total chaos, sin, and spiritual darkness, darker than anything we can imagine.

Living for ourselves causes us to confuse our values and to seek the wrong things. And when we live this way, we pay a high price to do so even though we may not realize how much it costs. We often pay a high price for a cheap thrill. But when we choose to give up selfish living with God's help, we find life on a higher level, and we are transformed into the image of Jesus Christ (Romans 8:29; 2 Corinthians 3:18).

This would be a good time to pause and seriously think about how selfish or unselfish you are. Talk to the Lord about it and ask Him to reveal truth to you. If you find that you are selfish, don't feel condemned. Instead, be joyful that you see something that can change in you as you work with the Holy Spirit to change it.

It is always important for us to realize that the path to living the great life God wants us to live is to deny ourselves, walk in love, and live unselfishly. Jesus tells His disciples, "If anyone intends to come after Me, let him deny himself [forget, ignore, disown, and lose sight of himself and his

> *The path to the life God wants us to live is to deny ourselves, walk in love, and live unselfishly.*

own interests] and take up his cross, and [joining Me as a disciple and siding with My party] follow with Me [continually, cleaving steadfastly to Me]" (Mark 8:34).

We often hear people say when they are having difficulty or have endured a tragedy in their life that the situation is just their "cross to bear." But pain and trouble do not represent the cross Jesus has asked us to carry. Our cross is to live an unselfish life—one in which we don't put ourselves first in everything but instead seek to be considerate of others and let them recognize our unselfishness. Pastor John MacArthur says, "The true gospel is a call to self-denial. It is not a call to self-fulfillment."[1]

Wherever you are in your process of learning to live unselfishly, keep in mind that if you seek God first, He will take care of you. Jesus says, "But seek first the kingdom of God and His righteousness, and all these things shall be added to you" (Matthew 6:33 NKJV). As long as we keep Him first in all things, He will provide everything else we need. Ask God for what you want, then leave the timing of it in His hands while you continue serving Him by helping others.

"But Really, What About Me?"

At this point, you may be thinking, *Okay, Joyce, I'm starting to see what you're saying. But really, what about me?* I think it is important to say that seeking a life of unselfishness does not mean you can never do anything you want to do or that all of your time and effort will be spent in serving others. God wants us to live balanced lives, and it is important that we take care of ourselves. If you don't take care of yourself, you won't be able to take care of anyone else. You will, of course, take care of yourself and do things you like to do; otherwise, you would be controlled by others, and that isn't right either. The key is to live a Spirit-led life. If you do, your life will be balanced.

> *A life of unselfishness does not mean you can never do anything you want to do.*

It's also important to say that living an unselfish life does not mean allowing others to use or abuse you. I have been used and abused, and I do not want anyone to put themselves in that position, thinking that doing so is "unselfish." I'm not talking in this book about becoming a doormat and letting people take advantage of you or manipulate you. I'm talking about healthy, godly ways of living the kind of unselfish life to which God calls us in His Word. This kind of living leads to joy and blessing, not to anything negative.

Philippians 2:4 says, "Let each of you esteem and look upon and be concerned for not [merely] his own interests, but also each for the interests of others." It doesn't say we can't think about our own interests, but we should not let them consume us. God knows what we long for, and Psalm 37:4 teaches us that if we delight ourselves in the Lord, He will give us the desires of our heart.

I repeat: *Don't let people take advantage of you.* Be a God-pleaser, not a people-pleaser. Some people, in their misguided efforts to be self-sacrificing, go too far in serving and end up resentful.

> *Be a God-pleaser, not a people-pleaser.*

I do things for myself, and I take care of myself. I do things I enjoy, and I spend some of my money on myself, but the difference between how I live now and how I lived previously is that now I am not totally self-absorbed. I don't put myself before everyone else, but neither do I put myself after everyone else. And, above all else, I seek to walk in love because Jesus says that the most important thing we can do is to love Him and love others as we love ourselves (Matthew 22:36–40). I often ask the Lord to show me what I can do for someone else. For example, I ask what I can do for my husband, for a friend, or for someone who works for me. He never fails to show me something, even if it's simply to give them a compliment.

I am a leader, and hundreds of people work for me. But I purposely engage in acts of service as an example to others and to remind myself that I am not any more important than anyone else. A true leader leads by example and not merely by words.

I work with the Holy Spirit to maintain balance in my life, balance between serving and doing for others and doing things for myself. I can sense when I need a break or when I just need to do something for myself. If we don't take those times, we will suffer burnout.

Some people feel guilty if they do anything for themselves, and this never ends well. It reflects more of a martyr mentality, serving others at your own expense, than a true servant's heart. Most people who live to help others and feel they don't deserve to do things for themselves talk frequently about all they do for others and how little they are appreciated. They also mention frequently that they put themselves last, and this makes me wonder if they are proud of it. Always putting yourself last is just as bad as always putting yourself first. Neither approach is a balanced way to live.

It is true that some people will take advantage of those who help them. But they do this because the helpers allow them to do so. I have learned that if someone is taking advantage of me, it is my fault for letting them do it. Letting people take advantage of you or control you is not only not good for you, but it's not good for them either.

Jesus says the one who serves is greatest of all (Matthew 23:11). Jesus Himself put on a servant's towel and humbly washed His disciples' feet as an example to us (John 13:5, 15). After this, He says to the disciples, "If you know these things, blessed and happy and to be envied are you if you practice them [if you act accordingly and really do them]" (John 13:17). Serving others doesn't sound as though it would make us happy, but Jesus says it will bring us joy. I have experienced this, and I know that it is true.

CHAPTER 2

Unexpected Joy

It is more blessed [and brings greater joy] to give than to receive.

Acts 20:35 AMP

If you were to ask ten people what they think would make them happy, they would probably think about what they want and tell you that getting it would make them happy. As human beings, we are wired to think about what we want. Our minds tend to default to what benefits us, not what's good for other people. We *think* we are blessed, which is one way of saying "happy," when we receive what we want, but as the opening scripture of this chapter states, we are actually more blessed when we give to others.

Not only do people naturally tend to think that getting what they want will make them happy, but the world reinforces this idea. Just think about some of the television commercials you have seen. Most of them are geared toward making you want something and telling you that you deserve to have it. Occasionally, especially during the holiday season, advertisements are geared toward giving fabulous gifts to other people. But most of the time, the world around us and the media that influences us push us to spend money on things that will make life easier or more convenient—or that will make us look better, feel better, perform better, be more comfortable, or have more fun.

Many people in our society have concluded that the way to be happy is to have what they want. But this isn't true. I have heard that some celebrities and other high-profile people have admitted that once they attained or accrued the things they wanted, their lives still felt empty. That's because getting what we want doesn't ultimately leave us satisfied in our souls or fulfilled in our hearts. It only leaves us wanting more.

The Reasons People Become Self-Focused

Why do we think getting what we want will make us happy? As I've mentioned, it's human nature. Plus, we are bombarded with this message through the media. But there are deeper reasons people become self-focused and greedy instead of unselfish and generous. Let's look at five of the key reasons and view them as joy-blockers, because they certainly prevent us from experiencing the joy God desires for us.

1. Emotional pain

Anytime we feel pain in our hearts, we tend to turn inward and focus on ourselves. Think about what happens when you get a paper cut. The sting of the cut on a very small part of one finger demands all your attention. Emotional pain works in a similar way. When you hurt, all you want is to feel better, and you devote your time and energy to helping yourself find relief from the pain. Many people seek that relief in purchasing something for themselves or going on a vacation they really cannot afford. Some even look for relief in eating, so they end up overeating and weighing more than they should. Then they don't like the way they look, and their misery is only made worse. Instead of finding ways to avoid the emotional pain, we can reach out to God and ask for His help in dealing with it.

2. Disappointment

Disappointment is certainly a type of emotional pain, but I think it's worth mentioning specifically because when people are disappointed, they often try to compensate for what they wanted and didn't get. They try to fill the void with something else, something they think will make them happy instead of sad. We may never be able to completely avoid disappointments in life, but we can choose how we react to them.

3. Lack

When people feel they lack something, they try to make up for it any way they can. They feel that if they don't have something, they need to find a way to get it. They often spend a lot of time and energy—and sometimes go into debt—to acquire whatever it is they feel they lack. When people have grown up in situations where they never had enough, they may go to extreme measures trying to acquire material things, positions, and/or power so they can feel assured they will never have to do without again.

4. Fear

When people are afraid or feel threatened in some way, they are totally focused on themselves. In fact, it's almost impossible to get ourselves off of our minds when we are fearful. We worry and pour our energy into hoping and praying what we fear will not happen or to trying to keep it from happening. When we have serious problems and feel afraid, the last thing we think about is doing something to help someone else.

5. Childhood issues

As a child, I experienced everything I have mentioned on this list, often to an extreme degree. I lived in constant emotional pain in many ways because of sexual abuse by my father and emotional abandonment by my mother. I was deeply disappointed by the way my parents treated me and by the fact that when I reached out for help, other people didn't want to get involved. I lacked the love, care, support, security, sense of value, and stability children need. In high school, I was not allowed to participate in extracurricular activities or have much interaction with my peers outside of school, so I lacked the social development opportunities that are so important for young people. I could go on and on about what I lacked in my childhood and how it led me to become a very selfish person for years. I also lived in intense fear, due to the abuse and my father's uncontrollable anger.

Your childhood experiences may have been different from what I lived through. Maybe you did not grow up with someone abusive, but the people around you did not model generosity or teach you the importance of expressing kindness toward others. Whatever the case, I do believe that what people learn and experience as children often leads them to selfish behavior.

The reasons for selfishness are many, and I have highlighted only five of the most common ones here. I encourage you to think and pray about them and see if any of them apply to you.

Self-focus steals the joy God wants us to have, so we need to deal with the joy-blockers in our lives. God will heal us from all our emotional pain and disappointment, and He will make up for anything we have lacked and always provide what we need. He will deliver us from fear, and He will heal and straighten out the childhood issues that affect us as adults. And if we let Him, He will teach us how to get our minds off of ourselves and experience the happiness that comes from thinking of others.

Selfishness is a common and age-old problem. We might even say it's inborn in human beings because it was present in the Garden of Eden. God has been dealing with it for centuries and leading people out of it into a life of joy and blessing.

Selfishness Started in the Garden

The first time we see selfishness in the Bible is in the Garden of Eden, so it's as old as humanity itself. As soon as people were created, selfishness started. Adam and Eve saw something and they wanted it, even though God had forbidden them to have it—to eat from the tree of the knowledge of good and evil (Genesis 2:16–17). Even though they could freely eat of all the other trees in the garden, they sinned by deciding to please themselves instead of God. They wanted the one thing God had told them they could not have without serious repercussions. They decided to disobey God, and because of their disobedience, sin entered the world.

In the garden, Satan appeared in the form of a serpent and tempted Eve, but he did not tell her what the consequences would be if she made the wrong choice (Genesis 3:1–5). She gave in to the temptation and then tempted Adam (Genesis 3:6). Since that time, every person has been born with a sin nature, which means we are born selfish. But thankfully, Jesus has paid the price to set us free; we only have to take advantage of the opportunity He has provided.

Today, we still sin when we please ourselves instead of obeying God. Proverbs 3:5–6 gives us great advice to help us avoid being selfish: "Trust in the Lord with all your heart, and lean not on your own understanding; in all your ways acknowledge Him, and He shall direct your paths" (NKJV). And James 4:1–2 teaches us that what leads to strife is the fact that we want certain worldly things and that when those desires go unfulfilled, we resent the people who have what we want. James concludes these verses by saying simply, "You do not have, because you do not ask." Instead of struggling trying to get things, we should ask God for them and trust Him to give us what is best for us in His perfect timing.

Saying no to yourself and yes to God is not always easy, but it is easier than living selfishly and caring only for yourself. That leads to a lonely, miserable life. We usually blame our misery on other people, expecting them to make us happy, but we need to remember that our happiness is our responsibility, not anyone else's.

Sow Happiness

If we want to be happy, we should invest in our own happiness. Let me explain. Throughout God's Word, beginning in Genesis 8:22, we read about a principle that has become known as the law of sowing and reaping. We also see metaphors used as a means to convey wisdom and truth, and one of them is the metaphor that teaches us that God's Word is a seed that goes into our hearts and that the harvest is the crop of blessings we reap when we obey it. This is important to understand when we read the Parable of the Sower, which Jesus tells in Mark 4. This story refers to God's Word as seed sown in various kinds of ground by the Sower, the Holy Spirit. The soil, or ground, in this metaphor is our hearts. If our hearts are hard, the seed won't take root in the soil. Or if we worry and are deceived by riches, this will choke the seed, and it won't bear fruit (Mark 4:18–19 ESV). Mark 4:14–15 also says that when the seed is sown, Satan comes immediately and tries to steal it. Our enemy, Satan, does not want us to learn and act on God's Word because He knows that if we learn and obey it, we will have amazingly wonderful lives.

In this book, I am asking you to let God's Word take root deep in your heart and to become obedient to it perhaps as you never have before. I invite you to surrender your life in order to serve God and others. Every time you do this, you plant a seed of happiness and reap a harvest of joy that will be almost more than you can take in. God wants to amaze you if you will simply let Him do it.

Commit Your Way

Are you the type of person who wants your own way? Maybe you don't like to admit it, but you know it's true. I admit that I wanted my way for many years, and I still do at times. It took me years, and a lot of God's help, to learn to respond in more mature ways— instead of becoming angry, giving someone the silent treatment, or feeling sorry for myself—when I didn't get what I wanted. That's why I still remember my first Bible, which I received as a gift from my mother-in-law when Dave and I married. It was a white King James Bible, and she wrote this scripture in the front of it: "Commit thy way unto the Lord; trust also in him; and he shall bring it to pass" (Psalm 37:5 KJV).

This was a great scripture for me, someone who spent a lot of energy trying to get my way. Although I didn't understand it at the time, and I doubt she understood how perfect it was for me, this verse has often come back to me because I needed to commit *my* way to the Lord often throughout the years, trusting Him to bring to pass what He wanted to do in my life instead of insisting on having what I wanted and trying to figure out how to get it. It took a while, but I am learning daily that committing my way to Him is vital if I want to live a happy, fulfilled life. I could write a whole book on the blessings of simply allowing God to have His way in your life, but I will just say that as you surrender to Him and obey His Word, I am confident He will bring to pass all the good things He wants to do in your life too.

> Make the change from putting yourself first to putting God and others first.

I sense in my heart that some of you who are reading this book are standing on the edge of greatness, and all you need to do is make the change from putting yourself first to putting God and others first.

PART 2

Getting Out of Your Own Way

CHAPTER 3
What Do You Want?

I delight to do Your will, O my God; yes, Your law is within my heart.

Psalm 40:8

We all want to get our own way. As I've said, it's human nature. But as I mentioned in the previous chapter, the Bible teaches that we are to commit our way to the Lord. In other words, if we want to be happy, we need to surrender what we want to what He wants and trust Him to do wonderful things in us, through us, and for us. He may give us what we want, but He may also give us something better—something we don't know how to ask for.

I noted in the introduction to this book that people who are selfish live their lives thinking, *What do I want? What do I think? How do I feel?* I call these the three key questions of selfishness, and I believe that anyone who can stop allowing these questions to rule their lives will be headed for a life of joy and blessing. As long as we live according to what we want, what we think, and how we feel, we get in our own way and block the joy God wants us to have. But with the Holy Spirit's help, we can get out of our own way and make room for the blessings He has for us.

Dealing with Desires

Dealing with desires—which is another way of saying "what I want"—was particularly hard for me. Let me explain why it was so difficult.

When I left home at age eighteen after being sexually abused by my father for many years, I thought I had left my problems behind me. I didn't realize until many years later that my problems were in my soul (my mind, will, and emotions) and I couldn't simply move away from them. I had to deal with them and let God heal my soul. What I wanted was mostly rooted in selfishness, my thoughts were selfish and unspiritual, and my feelings controlled me. I was unable to trust that anyone would not hurt me eventually, especially if I gave them any kind of control over me. I was so afraid of being hurt that I tried to control everyone in my life.

Growing up, I had never gotten what I wanted. I had to accept what my father wanted for me. My mother was weak and afraid of him, so she never stood up for me or for herself. I was born with a strong type A, choleric personality, and being forced to do things against my will was especially difficult for me and had long-lasting negative effects on me. It made me rebellious toward other authorities in my life later on, especially male authority.

My father was controlling, and whatever he wanted to do was what we did. I reached out to a few people asking for help concerning the sexual abuse, but nobody wanted to get involved. When I realized no one was going to help me, I decided I would survive until I could leave home, and promised myself that, once I got away from my father, I would never let anyone tell me what to do again.

The determination not to let anyone tell me what to do didn't work well because I discovered that we are confronted with authority no matter where we go. If you have a job, your employer is your authority. While driving, the speed limit is an authority. "No parking" signs are a form of authority. As Christians, God's Word is our authority.

Watchman Nee, a Chinese Christian who was a serious student of God's Word and wrote many wonderful books, writes in his book *Spiritual Authority*:

> If you ever once in your life meet authority you will then be able to see God's authority everywhere. Wherever you go, your first question will be: Whom should I obey, To whom should I hearken?[2]

The way I apply this quote in a practical way is to tell people that when we go into a room, our first job is to look around, find the person in authority, and decide to honor that authority.

Sadly, our society today is filled with rebellion against authority, and most people think they should be able to do whatever they want to do. God has given us free will, and we can do whatever we want to do, but what we choose to do may not turn out well for us if it is not God's will. Every action has a reaction, and it is important for us to remember that.

God wants us to use our free will to choose His will. He doesn't want puppets who have no choice but to follow Him. He wants us to *choose* to follow Him. Many people ask, "What is God's will for me?" We discover God's will in His Word. For example, 1 Thessalonians 5:18 says, "Give thanks in all circumstances; for this is the will of God in Christ Jesus for you" (ESV). If we start by obeying this one scripture, we will be further along than most people.

I hear myself complaining at times, and I know better. We all have much to be thankful for, but when we are full of self-will, it doesn't take much for us to complain if we don't get exactly what we want or if we are inconvenienced in any way. If we begin by doing what we know to be God's will for everyone, such as being thankful in all circumstances, He will reveal His specific will concerning specific situations. Maybe your call is to preach the gospel to the world, or maybe it is to be a stay-at-home mom—both are equally important. What we do is not nearly as important as doing what we do for the Lord (Colossians 3:23). We are all in ministry—not just those of us who have "Reverend" in front of their name. You may think that praying or reading your Bible is more spiritual than cleaning your house, but if you are following the Holy Spirit, everything you do becomes spiritual if it is done unto God. Ecclesiastes 3:11 says, "He has made everything beautiful in its time." There is a time to pray and a time to study the Word, but there is also a time when you need to do practical chores, and they can be done with joy if done unto the Lord.

> Whatever you do, work at it with all your heart, as working for the Lord, not for human masters, since you know that you will receive an inheritance from the Lord as a reward. It is the Lord Christ you are serving.
>
> Colossians 3:23–24 NIV

The Big Boss

Remember, the soul is composed of the mind, the will, and the emotions, but the will (our power to make choices) is what I call the big boss. Ultimately, we will do what we want to do if we want it strongly enough. Even if it isn't best for us, God will sometimes let us have it simply to help us see that it doesn't fulfill us and that being in His perfect will is better than being in His permissive will. Our will, the big boss, has the final vote on all decisions.

God's Word teaches us what is best for us, but God doesn't force us to obey it. We get to choose.

Do you want God's will? If so, you will have to die to self-will, and it will hurt. Perhaps you have a job that you really like, and you make very good money, but in order to keep that job you have to compromise your Christian principles. Your employer requires you to lie, cheat, and be generally dishonest to keep the job. Now you have a decision to make. Will you keep the job and continue compromising, or will you give the job up and trust God to get you one that is equal to or better than the one you currently have?

What if you decide to give up the job because of your love for God, but you cannot find a new one that pays as much as the current one does? Will you still be happy and content even if you must make some financial sacrifices in order to be in God's will?

Sometimes we don't know what a hold certain things have on us until we must do without them.

A man who works for us has a twenty-year-old daughter. She is deeply committed to God and will not compromise her morals. He told me that she is frequently not invited to activities and outings with her friends because they know she will not compromise. This hurts her, her dad says. It may hurt her now, but God will reward her, and she will be much happier than her friends who compromised.

I quit my job in the late 1970s in order to have time to study God's Word in preparation for the ministry I believed God was calling me to. I couldn't teach God's Word if I didn't know God's Word. I didn't quit my job because I wanted to, but I kept feeling strongly that God wanted me to leave it. For a long time, I was in disobedience and fear, and I didn't quit. I knew that if I did, we would be short forty dollars a month for our regular bills and have nothing for extra expenses such as clothes for the children, Dave, and me; medical expenses; car repairs; and other financial needs.

I did finally quit that job, but I got a part-time job. The second job didn't work out because God wanted Dave and me to depend on Him totally, even though my not working would leave us without the money we needed each month. In order for me to quit my job, we had to trust God totally to provide the rest of what we needed. It is not uncommon for people to try part-time obedience, but I can tell you from experience that it doesn't work. I got fired from my part-time job, even though I had held several jobs and never been fired before. I was a good employee and worked hard, but nothing I did at this part-time job worked because it was not God's will for me to have it.

> Doing God's will is not always comfortable, but it is always the best for you.

Doing God's will is not always comfortable, but eventually we will see that it is always the best for us. We will realize that what He asked of us had a purpose all along, even if we didn't understand it at the time. For six long years after I quit my job, our family lived month-to-month financially, needing a miracle each month to be able to fulfill our financial responsibilities and pay for other things we had to have. Those were difficult years, but now I look back at them with fond memories because God met our every need with His supernatural supply. People we didn't even know gave us money at times, or I found new shoes for my kids at garage sales for two dollars, or we got refunds we weren't expecting and didn't even know were due us. God did something different every time, but He always took care of us. Those were dark times for us, but God says that He will give us "the treasures of darkness" (Isaiah 45:3), and He certainly did. The miracles may seem small to you, but to us they were major. Over those six years, we learned to trust God for our provision, and I can't even begin to tell you how much that has helped us trust God for the large amounts of money now needed to run the ministry every month. Because we learned how to trust God for little things years ago, now we don't have any difficulty trusting God for big things. You may not understand something difficult you are going through now, but later on you may see how important it was. God doesn't waste anything in our lives, not even our pain if we will give it to Him.

> God doesn't waste anything in your life.

Those six years were painful yet wonderful at the same time. We didn't have everything we wanted, but we did have what we needed. God is good, and He will never let you down if you are walking in His will. When we do God's will, we may not always get what we want, but we will get what is best for us even if it doesn't seem so at the time. Those six hard years finally came to an end. God gave us more income, and we did not have to struggle as much. They were not the end of all difficult times we have faced, but I learned not to resist God's will so much, and that has lessened the pain of the difficult situations we have faced since then.

I have been walking with a friend through a hard time because she discovered her husband has been addicted to pornography throughout their marriage. She wants the marriage to work and so does he, so she is doing all she knows to do to cooperate with God's plan for their restoration. She said, "Joyce, the pain is so bad, I don't know if I can stand it." I gave her the same advice I am giving you: "Relax and breathe." I explained to her that the pain is digging a deeper place in her soul for God to fill. I also told her to stop trying to figure everything out and take it one day at a time. She and her husband both have problems from their childhood and are both in counseling. I am convinced that when this is all over, their marriage will be better than it ever has been before, but they have to go through the difficulty of the wilderness before they get to the joy of their Promised Land.

Jesus, Our Example

In Matthew 26 we see a powerful picture of Jesus' willingness to go to the cross because it was God's will, even though He didn't want to endure the agony. Verses 36–44 (NIV) depict what Jesus went through in Gethsemane:

> Then Jesus went with his disciples to a place called Gethsemane, and he said to them, "Sit here while I go over there and pray." He took Peter and the two sons of Zebedee along with him, and he began to be sorrowful and troubled. Then he said to them, "My soul is overwhelmed with sorrow to the point of death. Stay here and keep watch with me." Going a little farther, he fell

with his face to the ground and prayed, "My Father, if it is possible, may this cup be taken from me. Yet not as I will, but as you will." Then he returned to his disciples and found them sleeping. "Couldn't you men keep watch with me for one hour?" he asked Peter. "Watch and pray so that you will not fall into temptation. The spirit is willing, but the flesh is weak." He went away a second time and prayed, "My Father, if it is not possible for this cup to be taken away unless I drink it, may your will be done." When he came back, he again found them sleeping, because their eyes were heavy. So he left them and went away once more and prayed the third time, saying the same thing.

I think this passage is a wonderful example of what I am talking about in this chapter. Jesus, as the Son of Man, did not want to go to the cross and face the suffering He knew He would go through. But as the Son of God, He wanted God's will more than He wanted His own. He said His soul was "overwhelmed with sorrow to the point of death." In other words, what He was going through hurt so bad that He felt it might kill Him. Have you ever been going through something so difficult that you said, "I feel like this is going to kill me?" I have, yet I am still here and more alive than ever. Going through hard things does kill the flesh (our sin nature, expressed through our bodies, minds, wills, and emotions), but as the flesh

> As the flesh dies to self, you are made alive in the Spirit.

dies to self, we are made alive in the Spirit. First Peter 3:18 says this happened to Jesus: "For Christ also suffered once for sins, the righteous for the unrighteous, to bring you to God. He was put to death in the body but made alive in the Spirit" (NIV).

Jesus endured what He went through for us, even though His

flesh didn't want to. We can also do the will of God, even if we don't want to. Our flesh doesn't have to *want* to do what is right in order for us to do it. We are children of God, yet we are also children of the flesh. As we feed on God's Word, the Spirit becomes stronger than the flesh, and we can choose to do what God wants even though our flesh fights against it.

Consider these scriptures, and they will strengthen you in your war against the flesh:

> I pray that out of his glorious riches he may strengthen you with power through his Spirit in your inner being.
>
> Ephesians 3:16 NIV

> So then, those who suffer according to God's will should commit themselves to their faithful Creator and continue to do good.
>
> 1 Peter 4:19 NIV

> For it is better, if it is God's will, to suffer for doing good than for doing evil.
>
> 1 Peter 3:17 NIV

> You need to persevere so that when you have done the will of God, you will receive what he has promised.
>
> Hebrews 10:36 NIV

I want to encourage you to never give up. There will be hard times and perhaps even times when you just don't know if you can do what God is asking of you. But if you persevere, commit your way to the Lord, and want God's will more than you want your own, you will give glory to God, and He will reward you. You won't just read about His promises; you will receive them.

CHAPTER 4

What Do You Think?

For God has not given us a spirit of fear, but of power and of love and of a sound mind.

2 Timothy 1:7 NKJV

The second key question of selfishness is one people ask themselves often and one that guides our words and actions more than we may realize: "What do I think?" The mind must be renewed according to God's Word, and we will experience the "good and acceptable and perfect" will of God for our lives (Romans 12:2). When this happens, our mind becomes a powerful tool to help us break free from selfishness and enjoy the blessings of an others-focused life.

Our thoughts affect our will (decisions) and our emotions. The Bible says that we have the mind of Christ, and we can learn to think like He did (1 Corinthians 2:16). No one can force you to think a certain way. You can do your own thinking, and with God's help you can choose to think thoughts that will make your life better and make you happier, or you can think thoughts that will make your life miserable and cause you to feel discouraged and depressed. If you think positively and according to God's Word, you will have a positive and good life. But if you think negatively, you will not enjoy your life, and you will be unhappy.

I was in my forties before I learned that I could choose my thoughts. Prior to that time, I simply thought whatever fell into my mind. It was not until later in life that I learned that many of those thoughts were lies from the devil, lies intended to deceive me. If you currently have selfish and self-centered thoughts, you can replace them with thoughts focused on other people and on how you could help and encourage them. The more you do this, the happier you will be. For example, when I take time to plan something nice for someone, I feel more joyful in my spirit and soul. Thinking positive thoughts about other people is one way you can increase your joy anytime you want to. I have learned to listen to what people tell me they would like to have, and if I am able, I provide it for them, unless, of course, doing so would not be good for them.

"Let Me Tell You What I Think..."

If we listen to ourselves and other people, we often hear comments such as these:

- "Well, I think..."
- "Let me tell you what I think..."
- "In my opinion..."
- "Here's what I think..."

The problem with wanting to give our input is that what we think isn't always based on the truth of God's Word or accurate knowledge; we simply want people to think we know certain things, and we like to give advice and our opinion, even when no one asks for it.

Have you ever asked someone a question and, without taking time to think about it, they said, "Well, off the top of my head," and then proceeded to give you an opinion? The last thing we need is something off the top of anyone's head. We need direction from God. And if we are going to get advice, it needs to come from someone we believe has true knowledge of the subject. But due to pride, we all think we know a lot more than we actually do.

Sometimes, we critically judge people we don't know much about, and we can harm someone's reputation by spreading our thoughts and opinions around for others to hear. Many of our problems come from things we say that should not be said.

I think it's safe to say that our thinking and speaking are two of the most important

Thinking and speaking are two of the most important topics to study in God's Word.

topics to study in God's Word. If we think something and believe it, we will act accordingly—even if what we believe isn't true. When this happens, we are deceived. The devil is the great deceiver, and his goal is to get us to believe his lies and end up living miserable lives.

> Misery is almost always the result of thinking.
>
> —Joseph Joubert[3]

Joseph Joubert connects misery with thinking, but I would add that it is the result of *wrong* thinking. We must have our minds renewed by God's Word if we ever hope to experience God's will (Romans 12:2). We will have to die to our own thoughts and know that no matter what we think, if it doesn't agree with God's Word, then we are wrong, and God is right.

How Many Lies Do You Believe?

When we believe lies but don't know they are lies, it is very dangerous, because we live by what we believe, even if it isn't true. The more you study God's Word, the more you will know the truth, and the truth will defeat and replace the lies you may believe.

The devil also loves to plant prideful thoughts in our mind, and this often manifests in judging others or being critical of them. Pride also makes us easy to offend. If someone offends you and you think about the offense repeatedly, you will become angrier and angrier until you will probably let the anger explode out of your mouth toward the person who offended you or even toward others—maybe both. We desperately need peace in our lives, and, as Proverbs 13:10 says, "By pride comes nothing but strife" (NKJV). If you possess humility, you will realize that because you make mistakes also, you can choose to believe the best of a person who hurt you and forgive them. That's much easier than being angry and starting strife.

Mahatma Gandhi said, "A man is but the product of his thoughts. What he thinks he becomes,"[4] and I agree. I believed that because I had been abused, I would always have a second-rate life. But that was a lie the devil had told me for years. As I studied God's Word, I found out that God restores things and that, as His children, we become new creatures; old things pass away and all things become new (2 Corinthians 5:17 NKJV). I also learned that what David writes about God in Psalm 23:3 is true: "He restores my soul" (NKJV).

I believed nobody loved me, but that wasn't true, because God loved me. He always has and always will. When bad things happened to me, I thought God was punishing me for my sins, but the truth is that Jesus took my punishment when He died on the cross (Isaiah 53:5; Romans 4:25 NIV). Sins sometimes have consequences, but the consequences do not represent punishment from God; we bring them on ourselves through disobedience.

During my younger years I did not understand as much about God as I do now. When I sinned and repented, I still felt guilty and believed God was angry with me. But the truth is that when Jesus bore our sins, He also took the guilt that comes with them. When God forgives us, He forgets the sin and removes it as far as the east is from the west (Psalm 103:12; Isaiah 43:25 ESV).

For many years after I began teaching God's Word, I often believed my sermons were not good, especially if no one complimented me after I had taught. If anyone left the room while I was teaching, I was miserable because I believed they left because they didn't like me or my teaching. This may not have been true. Perhaps they ate something that didn't agree with them and needed to leave the room, or perhaps they had to go to work and really didn't want to leave.

If we watch people's faces or gauge their responses in order to determine whether we are doing well or not, we may never feel good about anything, because the devil can always find and draw our attention to the one person who appears bored or angry. Even if their feelings have nothing to do with us, we let their appearance or behavior determine how we feel about ourselves.

> Your thoughts affect every area of your life.

Our thoughts determine our level of confidence or lack of confidence. Indeed, our thoughts affect every area of our lives, and we must be attentive to them and diligent to make sure they agree with God's Word. I have been uncovering the lies of Satan for years through studying God's Word, and each one I uncover increases my freedom. I believe the same will happen for you.

Think on These Things

For the rest, brethren, whatever is true, whatever is worthy of reverence and is honorable and seemly, whatever is just, whatever is pure, whatever is lovely and lovable, whatever is kind and winsome and gracious, if there is any virtue and excellence, if there is anything worthy of praise, think on and weigh and take account of these things [fix your minds on them].

Philippians 4:8

If we could train ourselves to have only beautiful and excellent thoughts, our lives would be happier than we can possibly imagine. Our level of joy and peace is connected to our thoughts. Let me suggest twelve ways of thinking that will be beneficial to you.

1. No matter what kind of difficulty you are currently experiencing, always think and believe it will end well. Don't imagine the worst; believe the best. Be full of hope, which means expecting something good to happen.

2. Don't worry. That will only upset you more and do nothing to solve your problem. Anxious thoughts can be cast down, and you can choose to think about trusting God. Remember other times He has helped you.

3. When you think about people you know, don't think about their flaws. Instead, think about their strengths. Think of the qualities that you enjoy in them, not the ones that irritate you.

4. When you think about yourself, don't rehearse in your mind everything that you think is wrong with you. Instead, remember that you are God's child and that He loves you unconditionally. He created you, and He doesn't make mistakes. Think about your strengths and abilities rather than your faults.

5. Don't focus on past mistakes or painful things that have happened to you. Look to the future and believe God has good things planned for you.

6. Don't allow yourself to think self-pitying thoughts. Think about how blessed you are, not how mistreated you are. Don't think about what people *don't* do for you; instead focus on what they *do* for you.

7. Think about what you can do to help other people and make them happy.

8. Keep your mind on what you are doing and learn to be mentally present. I have a bad habit of doing one thing while thinking about the next thing, but God is helping me with this.

9. Let your mind be filled with thanksgiving. Think about everything you have to be thankful for; express your

thanks to God and to people who help you and do things
for you.

10. Don't compare yourself with others. Be yourself and don't
be jealous of what anyone else has or can do.

11. Have a humble mind, and don't think of yourself more
highly than you should (Romans 12:3). Instead, realize
that God's grace has endowed you with talents, abilities,
and gifts. According to Philippians 2:5–8, we are to let the
same mind that was in Jesus be in us. Although He was
equal with God, He was humble enough to make Himself a
servant to all and to be obedient enough to die on a cross to
save us from our sins.

12. Don't dread. We all have to do things that are not our favor-
ites, but dreading them only makes them worse. When you
have a task coming up and are not looking forward to it,
ask God to help you with it. Don't think about it until the
time comes to do it, then do it.

These twelve ways of thinking can transform your life. Renew-
ing the mind takes time and happens little by little, so you are
not likely to wake up tomorrow with a whole new mindset and be
able to sustain it. But you can commit to incorporating these ways
of thinking into your mindset and ask the Holy Spirit to help you.
You might even consider focusing on one of them each month for
the twelve months of the next year. That way, this time next year
you will have made great progress and helped build a strong foun-
dation for ongoing growth and change in the way you think.

Why? Why? Why?

We waste a lot of time trying to figure out why things happen the
way they do. We should replace our *why* thoughts with thoughts

of trusting God. The Bible is full of scriptures about trusting Him, and the more we study and meditate on them, the easier it will be to trust Him instead of reasoning within ourselves. One of my favorite passages is Proverbs 3:5–6:

> Lean on, trust in, and be confident in the Lord with all your heart and *mind* and do not rely on your own insight or understanding. In all your ways know, recognize, and acknowledge Him, and He will direct and make straight and plain your paths. (emphasis mine)

A pastor I know and respect lost his lovely wife to cancer. He has been a faithful and committed pastor for many years. He, his family, and the church prayed diligently for his wife to be healed, yet she died. The statement he made to God was "I will never ask You why," and then he prayed that God would help him handle the situation well so he could be a good example to his family, church, and friends. I thought that was absolutely wonderful and amazing. At a time when his own pain was devastating, he was thinking of others.

It isn't wrong to ask God why, but He doesn't always answer *why* questions. My guideline is this: I can ask why and reason until I start getting confused. Then I know I've gone too far, because confusion is not of God (1 Corinthians 14:33). There are many mysteries hidden in God, and things happen to us and others that we will not understand until we get to heaven. God desires that we trust Him completely, and we would not need to do that if we knew all the answers. Digging too deeply into why something happened can open the door to deception, which may eventually lead a person to begin to believe things about God that are not true. Never blame your problems on

God desires that you trust Him completely.

God, because He is not the author of our pain. Sin—whether it is personal sin or the effects of living in a sinful world—is the source of pain. If you are even the tiniest bit angry with God because you don't think something is fair, or because you don't understand something that has happened to you, ask Him to forgive you and remember that God is the One who *helps* you, not the One who *hurts* you.

Exalt God's Word over Your Own Thinking

To die to our own thinking means we do not exalt what we think above God's Word. If what I think doesn't agree with God's Word, then I die to my thinking and accept His Word as the truth. As I mentioned earlier, human nature is to enjoy thinking we know more than we actually do.

> Do not exalt what you think above God's Word.

Job suffered terribly and didn't think he deserved such distress, so he questioned God's justice and fairness. Job wanted to know why so many terrible things had happened to him.

In Job 38–41, God speaks of many mysteries in the universe and of the mighty things He has done, and Job finally realizes he has no right to question God. After God asks Job to answer His questions, which he was unable to do, Job says to the Lord:

> I know that You can do all things, and that no thought or purpose of Yours can be restrained or thwarted. [You said to me] Who is this that darkens and obscures counsel [by words] without knowledge? Therefore [I now see] I have [rashly] uttered what I did not understand, things too wonderful for me, which I did not know. [I had virtually said to You what You have said to me:] Hear, I beseech You, and I will speak; I will demand of

You, and You declare to me. I had heard of You [only] by the hearing of the ear, but now my [spiritual] eye sees You. Therefore I loathe [my words] and abhor myself and repent in dust and ashes.

Job 42:2–6

Like Job, we all have our own thoughts, and we are usually sure that whatever we think is right. But also like Job, we will eventually know that God is right in all He does. After Job repented and prayed for his friends, who blamed him for his problems, God gave Job twice as much as he had before (Job 42:10).

We should have reverence for God and know that He is never unjust. No matter what we may be tempted to think, we should die to our own thoughts and exalt God's thoughts, represented in His Word, above our opinions.

CHAPTER 5
How Do You Feel?

Whoever is slow to anger is better than the mighty, and he
who rules his spirit than he who takes a city.

Proverbs 16:32 ESV

The third key question we need to look at to move away from selfishness, toward others, and into greater freedom and joy is "How do I feel?" This is such an important question because emotions are strong, and if we follow them, we will end up with a lot of regret and sorrow.

> *If you follow emotions, you will end up with regret and sorrow.*

There are good emotions and bad emotions. We should learn to enjoy the good ones and not allow the negative ones to control us. We can't be led by how we feel, because feelings don't always tell us the truth about the situations we face. We may feel something is really terrible, when it may turn out to be good for us.

I firmly believe that emotions are the believer's number one enemy. I don't think I'm exaggerating to say that more than anything else people talk about with us, they talk about how they feel. They tell us how they feel physically, but they also tell us how they feel emotionally. I hear statements such as these, and I'm sure you do also:

- "I feel like no one loves me."
- "I feel guilty."
- "I feel like I don't fit in."
- "I feel insecure."
- "I feel like I'm not making any progress in overcoming my problems."
- "I feel discouraged."
- "I feel depressed."
- "I feel like giving up."

These statements and others like them represent negative emotions that will not produce good results if we follow them. In addition to that, they don't agree with God's Word.

Positive emotions are wonderful. They energize and motivate us. One day last week, I wasn't feeling up or down. It was just a normal day, and then I got some good news. A few minutes later, I got some more good news, and I felt happiness fill my soul. Times like these are great, but they don't happen every day, so we must learn to be satisfied with what I call "level emotion," meaning emotion that is neither up or down, but simply normal and stable. This is important because it is the way we will live most of our life. I have noticed two ways I can purposefully increase feel-good emotions: one is to be positive all the time, and the other is to think of what I can do for others. Both release joy in my life.

Personality plays a part in how we feel emotionally. I am serious-minded. I have a type A personality, and I am a goal-oriented, get-the-job-done-no-matter-how-I-feel type of person. Most of the time my emotions are just level, not up or down, but steady. I know how to have fun, but I am also very happy working, because accomplishment motivates me. There are times when my emotions are high, and even times when they are low, especially if I work too much and get too tired. But we all need balance in our lives. Otherwise, we will open a door to the devil to slip in and cause some kind of problem (1 Peter 5:8).

People with personality types different from mine, primarily those who are sanguine, are happy, upbeat, excited, and ready to have fun most of the time. We call them "the life of the party" because they bring fun with them wherever they go. They may tend to be undisciplined, and if they are not careful, they will make emotional decisions that will cause problems in their life. I used to think those people were more spiritual than I because they always seemed to be in a great mood and have high energy, while I was more serious-minded. But one of those high-energy people once told me, "Don't think I'm more spiritual than anyone else. This is just the way I was born, and my father was the same way." God makes us all different, and this is good, because we all need one another.

I know a woman who has extreme "up" emotions almost all the time, and she suddenly had a nervous breakdown because she never had taken the time to grieve any of the serious losses that had occurred in her life. Her happy attitude masked her pain at times. We were all shocked when she went from one extreme to the other, but this example is further proof that we need balance.

Paul writes in Philippians 4:11 that he "*learned* how to be content," whether he had an abundance or whether he lacked in some way (emphasis mine). In this verse, the Amplified Bible, Classic Edition describes *content* as "satisfied to the point where I am not disturbed or disquieted." I'm glad he said he *learned* to be content, because learning to deal with our emotions takes time and practice, and we usually have to go through several situations where we make bad decisions based on emotion rather than wisdom. After we've dealt with the fallout from those decisions, we learn not to trust our emotions.

Feelings Don't Always Tell Us the Truth

Feelings are fickle, and they don't usually notify us when they are going to change. They seem to have an energy of their own. We may go to bed feeling like doing something the next day, and when we get up the following morning, we don't want to do it at all. If people base their decisions on emotions, they can easily live without integrity or principle. God teaches us that it is very important for us to keep our word (Ecclesiastes 5:2, 4–5), yet many people in our society today do not take this principle seriously—partially because we make too many decisions based solely on emotion, and when our feelings change, we change with them, unless we learn to make right decisions no matter how we feel.

I have told people I would do things when my emotions were high, and later I did not want to do those things. But I have learned that it is not at all pleasing to God if I don't keep my word, so I do

> It is not at all pleasing to God if you don't keep your word.

what I said I would do, no matter how I feel about it. Psalm 15:4 casts a positive light on the person who "keeps an oath even when it hurts, and does not change their mind" (NIV). Can you think of commitments you have made—even seemingly minor ones—and still haven't fulfilled? If so, I highly recommend that you fulfill them or, at the very least, tell the people involved you are sorry you failed to keep your word.

Dominate Your Emotions

If we don't dominate our emotions, they will dominate us. Emotions are a strong force, and negative ones are often the culprits behind most of our sin. Emotions can cause people to have extramarital affairs and commit adultery. They often cause people not to finish what they start. And they can get many teenagers into types of trouble that often derail their future. Teenagers are especially vulnerable to emotions because they are feeling certain things for the first time, yet they are not usually mature enough to say no to feelings that will cause problems, because they have not had enough experience to understand them. If their parents teach them well, they may avoid making emotional mistakes, but if not, they may learn the hard way.

Some teens may so desperately want to be accepted by their peers

> *You may not be able to control how you feel, but you can control what you do.*

that they do things they know are wrong just to feel they are part of a group. This can be sad, because they often learn later that the people they tried so hard to please don't really care about them at all. People-pleasing in order to gain acceptance never ends well.

Just as you can control your thoughts, you can also control your emotions. You may not be able to control how you feel, but you can control what you do. You don't have to follow your emotions. I have written two books on emotions: *Managing Your Emotions*, which is out of print but available secondhand or perhaps at your library, and *Living beyond Your Feelings*, which I recommend you read if feelings are especially difficult for you to deal with.

Some people stuff their emotions down and pretend they are not a problem, but this can be more devastating than expressing them properly. We don't want to deny that we have emotions or merely try to ignore them; we simply want to refuse to let them control us. This will require help from the Holy Spirit, and He is more than willing to give us the help we need if we will ask Him. People who always follow their emotions will not walk in the Spirit. They will be soulish, carnal Christians.

Catering to the Flesh

To cater to the flesh means to do whatever our emotions want us to do, which is to follow them. Satan works through our emotions to control us and cause trouble in our lives. Romans 8:8 says, "So then those who are living the life of the flesh [catering to the appetites and impulses of their carnal nature] cannot please or satisfy God, or be acceptable to Him."

God is not pleased with a life lived by the flesh. He wants us to be led by His Spirit, because He will lead us into the good life that Jesus died for us to have. Paul writes in Romans 8:13–14:

> For if you live according to [the dictates of] the flesh, you will surely die. But if through the power of the [Holy] Spirit you are [habitually] putting to death (making extinct, deadening) the [evil] deeds prompted by the body, you shall [really and genuinely] live forever. For all who are led by the Spirit of God are sons of God.

God tells us that we have to put to death the dictates of the flesh. We do this by denying them the right to control us. If we give in to them, we feed them, and they remain strong. But you can kill anything by starving it. If we don't keep feeding harmful emotions, they will lose their strength and hold over us.

I remember all the times I felt sorry for myself each time I didn't get my way. When I did this, I continued to strengthen the emotion of self-pity. But when I began to deny it by praying my way through the disappointment of not getting my way, and trusting that God knew what was best for me, the emotion of self-pity slowly but surely lost its power over me. By the grace of God, I now rarely waste any time on feeling sorry for myself.

When we do what is right when we feel like doing what is wrong, we are growing spiritually and pleasing God instead of our flesh. Each time we do this, the real us (the spiritual us) grows stronger and the flesh grows weaker.

You are growing spiritually when you do what is right when you feel like doing what is wrong.

The amplification of 1 Corinthians 3:3 indicates that the Corinthians were "unspiritual" and had the nature of the flesh because they were "under the control of ordinary impulses." In other words, they were following their own desires (wills), thoughts, and emotions. They did what they *thought* was best, what they *wanted* to do, and what they *felt* like doing. This is what people do when they walk in the flesh; and they are the components of selfishness God wants us to be free from so we can live wholly for Him.

Each time we make a decision, we sow either to the flesh or to the spirit. If we sow to the flesh, we will reap ruin, decay, and destruction. But if we sow to the spirit, we will reap eternal life (Galatians 6:8).

I urge you not to live just for the moment, doing whatever feels good at the time. Instead, think of the future. What we do today determines how our future days will turn out.

If I become angry over something Dave says or does, I have only two choices: I can stay angry and ignore him or argue with him, or I can forgive Him and pray and trust God to help us deal with the situation as two mature adults.

> Satan gains more ground in the believer's life through unforgiveness than anything else.

Forgiving someone when you feel angry isn't easy. It requires a decision and the strength of God to help you bring the decision to fruition. I believe Satan gains more ground in the believer's life through unforgiveness than through anything else. It is sad how many Christians are angry with someone and hold unforgiveness toward them in their heart.

We can probably always think of someone we can be angry with if we live by our emotions, but this is an unpleasant and dangerous way to live. Why is it dangerous? According to Ephesians 4:26–27, anger can give the devil a foothold in our lives. In addition to that, according to 2 Corinthians 2:10–11, we should forgive to keep the devil from gaining an advantage over us. When God tells us to forgive, it is for our benefit. We are set free from the pain our enemies have caused when we let it go and trust God to bring justice into our lives.

When I Want to Do Good, Evil Always Comes

In Romans 7:15–8:1, Paul talks about wanting to do what was right, but doing what was wrong instead. This was confusing to him, and I think we can all relate to that. It is frustrating when we want and plan to do what is right, yet we end up doing what is wrong. I have often said that I can lie in bed in the mornings and plan for holiness all day, and it works until I put my feet on the floor. But soon, my plan for holiness no longer works.

We ask ourselves, as Paul must have, "What is wrong with me?" He went on to say that if he did what he didn't want to do, he really wasn't doing it, but that the sin dwelling within him was doing it. The amplification of Romans 7:20 calls it the "sin [principle]" that was "operating in my soul."

At this point, we can become confused if we don't understand what Paul meant. He was talking about his new nature—his inner being, which had been recreated in Christ—and his old nature, which, although crucified with Christ doctrinally and positionally, was still clinging to his flesh and causing him to do what he didn't want to do. We will never be completely free from the flesh until we die, but we can keep improving all the time.

Paul concludes this section of Romans by saying he was a wretched man and asking who would deliver him from the body of death that was giving him trouble. Then he answers his own question with some wonderful news for all of us. He writes, "O thank God! [He will!] through Jesus Christ (the Anointed One) our Lord!" (Romans 7:25). He finishes by saying in Romans 8:1, "There is therefore now no condemnation to those who are in

Christ Jesus, who do not walk according to the flesh, but according to the Spirit" (NKJV).

When we fail to do what is right, we can handle it either by continuing to walk in the flesh or by walking in the Spirit. If we walk in the flesh, we will feel guilty of wrongdoing, and all guilt does is drain us and render us ineffective for God's use. But if we handle our wrongdoing according to the Spirit, we confess our sin and trust God to change us, knowing that we cannot change ourselves by our own efforts. We let go of the past and move forward to what lies ahead (Philippians 3:13).

There is a big difference between weakness and wickedness. Paul was still weak in areas, but he was not wicked. He wanted more than anything to do God's will at all times. Many people

> There is a big difference between weakness and wickedness.

today have the same desire, and thankfully, God sees our hearts. Sanctification is an ongoing process that works in us throughout our lives, little by little, making us more like Jesus. While we are changing, we can still enjoy a wonderful life with God through Christ. We don't have to live in guilt and condemnation because "the law of the Spirit of life in Christ Jesus," which is in us, sets us "free from the law of sin and death" that tries to hold us captive (Romans 8:2 NKJV).

John Newton, an English slave trader who was transformed by Christ, said it well: "I am not what I ought to be, I am not what I want to be, I am not what I hope to be in another world; but I am not what I once used to be, and by the grace of God I am what I am."[5]

When Jesus comes back for us at the last trumpet call, we will all be changed in the twinkling of an eye (1 Corinthians 15:51–52). I think this means that anything that is still not sanctified in us will be perfected at that time. That will be a glorious day, and

I look forward to it. But until it comes, I will do my very best to not allow what I want, think, and feel to control me. And when I make mistakes, I will ask for and receive God's gracious forgiveness. Like a toddler learning to walk, when I fall, I will get up and try again.

PART 3

Becoming an Obedient Follower of Jesus

CHAPTER 6

Walking in the Spirit, Part 1

I say then: Walk in the Spirit, and you shall not fulfill the lust of the flesh.

Galatians 5:16 NKJV

The idea of walking in the Spirit is important to understand if we want to live the kind of unselfish life God desires us to live. It means surrendering our hearts and minds to God's Spirit, allowing Him to lead us, and obeying His promptings so we will not gratify the lust or desires of our flesh. I believe it's important to say here that walking in the Spirit isn't something we can do automatically simply because we are believers. It's something we must seek with ardent zeal, pray about, learn, and practice. As believers, we do have within us the ability to walk in the Spirit, and the Holy Spirit will help us do it and teach us how to live the new life we are meant to live. However, it is a process and takes place little by little as we grow spiritually. I encourage you to be patient and learn to enjoy the journey.

> If you are doing the right thing, your life has no room for the wrong thing.

Most of us wrestle with our temptations and problems, thinking that if we can defeat them, we will be able to live in a godly way. Galatians 5:16 says the opposite. It teaches us to focus on walking in the Spirit—and *then* we will not fulfill the desires of the flesh. If we are doing the right thing, there is no room in our life for the wrong thing. If we think about good things, there is no room in our mind to think about bad things. Susan's story makes this point well:

Susan's Story

I was in addiction for thirty years. I was a functioning addict. I worked, but any life outside of my work focused on me. When you're an addict, your life revolves around getting high. I don't know any addict that doesn't think about themselves excessively. You just want to feel better, but you never feel better because of the guilt and shame of getting high, so it's a vicious cycle.

When I gave my life to Christ and accepted His love for me, He not only set me free from my addiction, but He taught me an important lesson about love for other people. Had I not developed a lifestyle of helping others, I could have fallen back into addiction. God knew I had to get my mind off myself and onto others to live the life I'm living today. I realize now that the number one reason for staying in bondage is keeping your mind on yourself too much.

God has taught me that it's not all about me and shown me the importance of realizing that He is God and that He loves me. I'm important to Him, and other people are just as important to Him. I am to love those people as He loves them and to try to bring honor and glory to Him through the way I act toward others.

I started jail ministry about three years into my salvation. I felt God called me to serve in this way, even though I have never been incarcerated. Because of my battle with addiction, I can relate to the women in jail and often understand what leads to their time behind bars. I would say that 90 percent of the women I talk to deal with substance abuse.

So many people in this world just need a helping hand. They need someone to help. What I have, I have because God has blessed me, and so, with that, I want to bless others the best way I can.

The Struggle to Resist the Flesh

Derek Prince said, "Endeavoring to live the Christian life by your own efforts is the greatest single hindrance to walking in the Spirit."[6] When we try to live as Christians by our own efforts, we are living according to the flesh. We are relying on what we can do in our human abilities and strength, not on what God can do by His Spirit. This is exactly what I did for many years, and many people who want to live to please God attempt to do it too.

God says, " 'Not by might nor by power, but by My Spirit' " (Zechariah 4:6 NKJV). We cannot resist the flesh through our own effort. Another way to say this is "We cannot resist the flesh by the power of the flesh." We need the Holy Spirit's help (Romans 8:26). We must humble ourselves under God's mighty hand, remembering that "God resists the proud, but gives grace to the humble" (1 Peter 5:5 NKJV) and believing that in due time He will exalt us (1 Peter 5:6). Always ask God to help you, and when you have experienced victory, always thank Him for His help.

> You cannot resist the flesh through your own effort.

For a long time, when I faced obstacles as I tried to do what I thought God wanted me to do, I thought the devil was resisting me, trying to prevent me from being successful. This was confusing to me. I kept wondering why God wasn't helping me obey Him. The reason was that I had not asked Him to help me. I was relying on my own effort, not on Jesus, who says, "Apart from me you can do nothing" (John 15:5 NIV). Then I finally saw that *God* resists the proud. I was full of pride, and God wasn't going to help me until I humbled myself and asked Him for the help I needed. James 4:2 says, "You do not have, because you do not ask." I am sure we would be amazed if we knew what we are missing out on simply because we don't ask.

As we resist the flesh and walk in the Spirit, we can do as 1 Peter 5:7 teaches us and cast our care on God and He will care for us. This includes the care (anxiety, worry) of molding ourselves into the image of Jesus Christ. We should cast our *care* on God but not our *responsibilities*. We should always do what we can do, but not try to do what only God can do.

Peter goes on to write:

> And after you have suffered a little while, the God of all grace [Who imparts all blessing and favor], Who has called you to His [own] eternal glory in Christ Jesus, will Himself complete and make you what you ought to be, establish and ground you securely, and strengthen, and settle you.
>
> 1 Peter 5:10

Why do we have to suffer before God makes us what we ought to be? Even after asking for God's help, we usually have to wait for a while—and that's when we suffer. This helps us learn to lean on God sooner the next time we encounter a similar situation. Only God

> *Real change happens from the inside out, not from the outside in.*

can change people, because real change happens from the inside out, not from the outside in.

We can control our behavior to a certain degree, but until our heart's desires change, we will always struggle with the flesh. Struggle is not God's desire for us; His desire is for us to rest in Him. When we initially come to Jesus and desire to walk in the Holy Spirit, He slowly and strategically begins to show us the behaviors that need to change. He knows the perfect timing in our lives to bring these needed adjustments to our attention. You could probably name something right now that God is dealing with you about. The sooner you submit to Him, the happier you will be. He doesn't start working in our lives until we surrender to His will and ask Him to help.

God's Word is like a mirror. The more we look into it, the more we see our behavior in light of Jesus' behavior. I can have dirt all over my face and not know it until I look in the mirror, and this is the way God's Word works. It shows us what we should and can be in comparison to what we are presently. This is not so we can feel condemned, but so we can be convicted and then repent and ask God to change us. Always remember that guilt and condemnation are useless; they accomplish nothing.

God does change us, but change is a process, and one we must be patient with because it doesn't happen immediately. Once we turn something over to God, we need to trust that He is taking care of it and give it no more thought. God wants us to believe what He promises before we see it, so believe that God is changing you. He changes us little by little or, as 2 Corinthians 3:18 teaches, "from one degree of glory to another." I have reached the point where I genuinely appreciate the conviction (being made aware of sin) of the Holy Spirit. I am grateful that God loves me too much to leave me the way I am. I want to keep growing, and conviction is part of the process.

Let's say I tend toward jealousy, and I recognize this feeling as sin and repent, asking God to change me. Since the change won't happen right away, each time I am tempted to be jealous, I simply need to say, "Lord, I know You are working on this, and I am trusting You to change me." I can resist the temptation, but I cannot change the desire to be jealous, because only God can change my heart—and He will. We can even declare, according to God's Word, "I walk in love, and I am not jealous." Declaring our faith based on His Word is a good thing to do.

Something that has been effective for me when I struggle with jealousy or unforgiveness toward someone is to do something nice for them, perhaps to give them a compliment or a gift or do a favor for them. Good always overcomes evil (Romans 12:21), and reaching out in love toward someone who has hurt you is the best way to break the power of ill feelings toward them. Praying for them also helps tremendously. It is hard to stay angry or jealous of someone when you are praying for them.

I recall a woman who had hurt me deeply. She had actually been working behind my back trying to get me removed from a teaching position I held at my church so she could have it. Her efforts were not successful, but seeing her in church week after week and not having negative feelings toward her was very difficult for me. Time went by, and I kept fighting the anger and resentment I felt toward her. Then God put on my heart the idea of giving her a possession I was fond of and didn't want to give away, especially not to her. It took a while, but eventually I obeyed God, and the gift of giving broke the power of the sin of anger and resentment in me. Once this happened, I felt free.

God's Word is like medicine, and I highly recommend that you don't just read it randomly. Of course, you can follow a daily reading program if you want to, and doing so is a good discipline, but when you are struggling with a particular sin, study what the Bible says about that specific topic. Think of it this way: If you have a headache, you don't put a bandage on your head, and if you cut your finger, you don't put an aspirin on it. We know how to treat our physical bodies to help them heal, but sadly we often don't know how to doctor our souls. God's Word is medicine for our souls. If you are angry, studying success won't help you; study anger and forgiveness. If you are jealous, studying the creation account won't help; you should study everything you find on jealousy and envy.

Cooperating with the Holy Spirit

We trust God to do the work of changing us through the power of the Holy Spirit working in us, but we are responsible for cooperating with Him.

A. B. Simpson wrote in his book *Walking in the Spirit*:

> While we recognize the sovereign power of the Holy Ghost, visiting the heart at His pleasure, and working according to His will upon the objects of His grace, yet God has ordained certain laws of operation and cooperation in connection with the application of redemption; and He Himself most delicately recognizes His own laws and respects the freedom of the human will; not forcing His blessings upon unwilling hearts, but knocking at the door of our heart, waiting to be recognized and claimed, and then working in the soul as we heartily cooperate, hearken, and obey. *There is, therefore, a very solemn and responsible part for every man in cooperating with, or resisting and hindering the Holy Spirit.*
>
> "The manifestation of the Spirit is given to every man to profit withal" [1 Corinthians 12:7 KJV], that is to say, *it rests with the man who receives the first movement of the Holy Spirit to determine how far he will embrace his opportunity, cooperate with his heavenly Friend, and enter into all the fullness of the good and perfect will of God.*[7] (emphasis mine)

It is important to understand that even though we turn a situation over to God, we still have a responsibility to work with the Holy Spirit as He leads and guides us. I find that when I pray and need to hear from God about a situation, He often shows me something specific I need to do. Sometimes I may need Him to do a miracle, but sometimes He shows me something specific that I can do for myself. If I am willing to do it, He then gives me the power to follow through with it.

> *Even though you turn a situation over to God, you still have responsibility.*

Let me say again that we cannot change ourselves. It is God who changes us through the working of His Word and the Holy Spirit. Our part is to study God's Word and cooperate with the Holy Spirit, obeying what He leads us to do.

CHAPTER 7

Walking in the Spirit, Part 2

If we live in the Spirit, let us also walk in the Spirit.

Galatians 5:25 NKJV

Walking in the Spirit does not come with a list of rules to follow; it is something we do based on how He leads us at any given time. The best way to know what the Holy Spirit approves of is to learn to follow peace (Romans 14:17). If what we are doing is right for us at the time, we will have a peaceful calm and quiet inside of us, but if it isn't right, we will sense a gentle pressure that does not feel pleasant. The Holy Spirit doesn't yell; He whispers.

For example, if I am with a friend and start to gossip about another friend, I immediately start feeling uncomfortable inside. I can continue gossiping while being uncomfortable, but then I am not being led by the Spirit. Instead, I am following my own will, doing what I want to do. I won't be happy with myself later and will feel guilty. I will eventually repent, and God will forgive me, but I will have to battle guilt before finally feeling free and peaceful. I will also be disappointed in myself because I didn't do what was right to begin with. The solution to this kind of problem is easy: Just obey right away and avoid the misery.

When I am watching television, many times I am interested in what I'm watching, then something comes on that is unsuitable for me to watch, and I immediately feel uncomfortable. I admit it is often hard to obey that nudge from the Holy Spirit and turn off the show because I am caught up in the mystery or the story. But after years of doing things my own way, I now know that continuing to do something when I sense the conviction of the Holy Spirit is not worth it.

Being led by the Spirit doesn't mean He gives us minute-by-minute instructions about what we are to do. In many situations, we are free to make our own decisions and trust that if we make a wrong one, He will let us know. I asked the Lord this morning what He wanted me to do today and didn't get any specific answer, so I decided I would go shopping. Then the person I had planned to go with had a change of plans and could not go, so I decided to stay home and work on this book. In this instance, my circumstance showed me what God's will was. God often speaks to us through circumstances. He opens and closes doors to show us what to do.

Following the leading and prompting of the Holy Spirit is what enables us to be changed into the image of Jesus Christ, becoming more like He is. But as I have mentioned, we must be patient in this process, because it usually takes several rounds of failing before we begin to recognize how the Holy Spirit works to bring about the changes God knows we need.

> *Follow the prompting of the Holy Spirit to be changed into the image of Jesus Christ.*

Enjoy Yourself While You Change

While you are changing, you don't have to be angry with yourself or reject yourself. You can enjoy where you are on the way to where you are going. God sees the way you are now, but He also sees what you will become, and He treats you as though you have already arrived. When I first began to teach a Bible study in my home, I did so wearing short shorts and smoking cigarettes. Ordinarily, people might think, *God can't use someone in that condition.* But He did use me, because not only did He see where I was, He also saw where I would eventually be. At the time, I had no idea that the way I dressed or the smoking set a poor example for others. The people coming to the Bible study did the same things. After a while, I began to feel convicted that my outfits were improper and my smoking habit was unhealthy, so I changed my dress, and God helped me stop smoking. Our Father sees us in and through Christ if we have put our faith in Him. Second Corinthians 5:21 explains how God views us:

> For our sake He made Christ [virtually] to be sin Who knew no sin, so that in and through Him we might become [endued with, viewed as being in, and examples of] the righteousness of God [what we ought to be, approved and acceptable and in right relationship with Him, by His goodness].

Once we are born again (receive Jesus as our Lord and Savior), God views us in and through Him. It is very important for us to learn to know who we are in Christ so we can begin to understand how He sees us. God loves us and wants us to love ourselves in a balanced way, and as long as we don't love ourselves, we won't be able to love other people.

Perhaps the idea of loving yourself sounds strange to you, but in reality, you are loving the you that God made with His own hands in your mother's womb (Psalm 139:13–16). You are loving the you that you were prior to sin, and you are loving the you that you're in the process of becoming again. Thankfully, God looks at our heart and considers that, not just our actions. If your heart's desire is to live as God calls you to live, He will help you get there.

Jesus says we should love our neighbor as we love ourselves (Matthew 22:39). If we are to love our neighbor (other people) as we love ourselves, how can we do it if we don't love ourselves? We can't. I often say that we cannot give away what we don't have.

I encourage you not to think so much about what is wrong with you. Recognize your faults, but don't focus on them endlessly. Instead, see and celebrate the progress you have made. Appreciate the gifts, talents, and abilities God has graciously put within you, and enjoy the life He has given you.

The Difference between Spirit and Flesh

Both the Holy Spirit and the flesh are characterized by certain types of behavior. The better we understand this, the more effectively we can walk in the Spirit. Let me point out several differences between the Spirit and the flesh:

- The Holy Spirit leads, guides, and prompts. *To prompt* means "to move to act, spur, incite; to give rise to, inspire; to assist with a reminder, remind."[8] The flesh manipulates, controls, demands, and pressures.
- The Holy Spirit is humble, gentle, meek, and lowly. The flesh is harsh, hard, sharp, and pressing.
- The Holy Spirit speaks truth. He leads and guides us into all truth (John 16:13) and brings clarity. The devil is a deceiver, a liar, and a thief. He works through our flesh by tempting us to do things that are not God's will.
- The Holy Spirit, though He is God Himself and part of the Trinity, is submissive to the authority of God the Father and to Jesus. The flesh is rebellious.
- The Holy Spirit is faithful. He is committed, long-suffering, enduring, and patient. The flesh is impatient, uncommitted, unfaithful, and gives up easily when results are not immediate.
- The Holy Spirit is just. He shows no partiality or favoritism. He represents the God of justice. The flesh is unjust and dishonest.
- The Holy Spirit is excellent. He never compromises but always does exceedingly, abundantly above and beyond what we can think. He goes the extra mile. The flesh compromises and is mediocre at best.
- The Holy Spirit is merciful and forgiving. The flesh is unmerciful, judgmental, critical, and unforgiving.

- The Holy Spirit is generous. He loves to give and rejoices in the prosperity of God's children. The flesh is stingy, resentful, jealous, and envious.
- The Holy Spirit delights to see believers enjoy themselves and the life Jesus died to give them. The flesh steals true joy and attempts to replace it with self-centered fun.
- The Holy Spirit convicts but never condemns. The flesh makes us feel guilty, blames, gives a false sense of excessive responsibility, and condemns.
- The Holy Spirit is holy, righteous, and pure. The flesh is unholy, wicked, evil, impure, and unrighteous.
- The Holy Spirit loves. The flesh hates and is bitter, resentful, and easily offended. The flesh also holds grudges.

Of course, this list could go on, but it highlights several important distinctions between the Holy Spirit and our flesh. Without even being told what is right and what is wrong, most of us could recognize the fruit of either the Spirit or the flesh. After we are born again, we have an inner sense of right and wrong because the Holy Spirit lives in us. Then we simply need to start making choices that align with the Spirit.

A walk consists of many steps, and walking in the Spirit involves making many daily decisions and exercising self-control. I recently read that self-control is the highest form of self-love. When we control ourselves with God's help, we make the decisions God desires us to make, ones that will work out best for us and give us the best life possible.

The Fruit and Gifts of the Holy Spirit

The Bible teaches us about the fruit of the Spirit and the gifts of the Spirit, both of which are invaluable to believers in our everyday lives.

The apostle Paul lists the fruit of the Holy Spirit in Galatians 5:22–23:

> But the fruit of the [Holy] Spirit [the work which His presence within accomplishes] is love, joy (gladness), peace, patience (an even temper, forbearance), kindness, goodness (benevolence), faithfulness, gentleness (meekness, humility), self-control (self-restraint, continence). Against such things there is no law [that can bring a charge].

Those who are in Christ are distinguished from unbelievers in that we have been gifted with the Holy Spirit, who enables us to bear fruit (be productive and make a difference). I like to remind people that we are called to bear fruit, not merely to be busy. It is wise to stop occasionally and take an inventory of what we spend our time doing and ask ourselves if it is bearing good fruit or simply keeping us busy and often distracted from doing what truly benefits us and others. The fruit of the Spirit enables us to love and be kind to others instead of being selfish and self-centered.

> *You are called to bear fruit, not merely to be busy.*

Paul writes about the gifts of the Holy Spirit in Romans 12:6–8:

> Having gifts (faculties, talents, qualities) that differ according to the grace given us, let us use them: [He whose gift is] prophecy, [let him prophesy] according to the proportion of his faith; [he whose gift is] practical service, let him give himself to serving; he who teaches, to his teaching; he who exhorts (encourages), to his exhortation; he who contributes, let him do it in simplicity and liberality; he who gives aid and superintends,

with zeal and singleness of mind; he who does acts of mercy, with genuine cheerfulness and joyful eagerness.

Simply put, the gifts of the Spirit mentioned here are:

- prophecy
- practical service
- teaching
- exhortation (referred to as "encouragement" in the New International Version of the Bible)
- contribution (referred to as "giving" in the New International Version)
- giving aid and superintending (referred to in terms of leadership in the New International Version)
- acts of mercy

First Corinthians 12:4–11 (NKJV) lists additional spiritual gifts:

- word of wisdom
- word of knowledge
- faith
- gifts of healings
- working of miracles
- prophecy
- discerning of spirits
- different kinds of tongues
- interpretation of tongues

God distributes many different spiritual gifts in addition to the list found in Romans 12 and 1 Corinthians 12. Every person is gifted in some way or several ways. Some people are gifted musicians, artists, mathematicians, doctors, organizers—and the list goes on. Certain people are gifted to work with children, and others with individuals who have special needs. Even the people we see washing windows on high-rise buildings are surely gifted by God so they are not afraid of such heights. God has someone who is gifted to do every job that needs to be done.

Stay in Your Lane

If you stay in your own lane when driving a car, you will most likely be safe. But if you veer into someone else's lane, you could easily have a wreck. Life can be like this when we try to do things we are not gifted to do. People often waste years in frustration because they try to be someone they are not or do things they don't have the talent to do. When we stay within our giftings, we express them with ease because the Holy Spirit helps us. But He will never help us be someone else or do something we are not intended to do. Each of us simply needs to graciously do our part.

Paul teaches us in 1 Timothy 4:13–16 to give ourselves to our gift, whatever our gift or gifts of the Spirit may be. In other words, we should focus on the gifts God gives us. I focus on writing and teaching God's Word because I am a Bible teacher. I also have the gift of giving or contributing. Even though I always had the gift of giving, the Holy Spirit had to teach me how to use it to glorify God and not to gain attention for myself. I tried singing one time, and our sound people turned off my microphone during the worship in our conferences because I sing off-key. I tried learning to play a musical instrument and could not master that. I tried a lot of things that didn't work until I learned the hard way what I am sharing with you now. Save yourself a lot of trouble and personal pain by using the gift God has given you instead of trying to do something just because someone else is doing it. You don't need to compare yourself with anyone else or compete with them. You are free to be you!

When we walk in the Spirit, we don't live selfishly and fulfill what our flesh wants to do. Instead, we allow the Holy Spirit to empower us, we live loving, generous, unselfish lives, and life develops an ease and a flow that makes it enjoyable. Learn to follow the guidance of the Holy Spirit, and start enjoying your life more than ever before.

Lessons from the School of the Holy Spirit

There was a time in my life that felt like I was in school and the Holy Spirit was my teacher. As I learned to walk in the Spirit, He taught me many lessons, using the practical, ordinary activities of my life as our classroom. He is still teaching me today, but I would like to share some of the lessons I learned in the early days of walking in the Spirit, because He may want to use the everyday aspects of your life to help you learn to walk with Him too.

When I entered what I call the school of the Holy Spirit, He began showing me little things I did that were not right. One of them was not putting my grocery cart in the area marked "Please return carts here" when I finished shopping. I didn't want to make the extra effort to walk to that area, so I did what most people do and propped it somewhere, hoping it would not roll away. Often, I worked longer to balance the cart so it wouldn't roll away than I would have had I simply put it in the area designed to hold the carts.

Here's what's interesting: Although this was a simple thing, it took me *two full years* to reach the point where I was obedient every time and did as the Holy Spirit asked. I had many excuses: "Everyone else leaves their cart out in the lot, so why shouldn't I?" "This is what we pay the employees for; let one of them do it." "It's cold outside." "It's hot outside." "It's raining." "I'm in a hurry."

You may be thinking, *Really, Joyce? Did God actually deal with you about your grocery cart?* He did! Putting the cart where it goes seems to be such a little thing, but not doing it shows a lack of integrity. In addition, it isn't loving, because it is not what I would want customers to do if I owned the store. I was reminded that we are to do unto others as we want them to do unto us (Luke 6:31). I just didn't want to put my cart back! My flesh finally died, at least in this one area, and now I put the cart where it goes every time, and so do a lot of other people who listen to my teaching. You see, if we won't obey God in little things, we won't obey in big things, either.

> *If you don't obey God in little things, you won't in big things, either.*

When God called me into the ministry, I wasn't in a position to go to Bible college, but the Holy Spirit taught me in my daily life through ordinary chores. Here's another grocery store lesson. For years, our family lived on a tight budget, and often by the time I reached the last aisle, my calculator told me I had exceeded my budget. I started selecting items I could do without, but instead of putting them back where I got them, I routinely left them on the nearest shelf until I heard the Spirit whisper in my heart that I should put each one back where I got it. This lesson also took a long time to learn. I had excuses: "I'm already late and don't have time to put them back." "I can't remember where I got them." God was using these daily events to teach me integrity, meaning honesty, excellence, and moral strength. Sadly, integrity is something that is missing today in many people's lives. Some people don't even know what the word means.

The Holy Spirit taught me to keep my word, to hang up clothes other people had knocked off the racks while shopping, and to always tell the truth, even if it caused me personal pain. The lessons like these I have learned over the years are numerous. God has called us to be excellent, not mediocre. Mediocrity is halfway between success and failure. We are to do more than enough, not barely enough to get by. We all have an individual, secret relationship with God and should be committed to doing what He tells us to do, whether it is big or little, and doing it simply because we love Him. This helps us develop a relationship in which God becomes part of everything we do.

The devil is our enemy and God's enemy. His goal is to prevent God's children from living the wonderful life that Jesus died for us to have. He does this by deception and telling us lies we usually believe until we learn the truth from God's Word. I believed a lot of lies the devil told me, and they prevented me from enjoying God's best. Over a period of years, I learned to think differently about the little things in life because I realized that, to God, they were big things. Part of walking in the Spirit is to view things as God views them.

About forty-five years ago, I was leaving a store and noticed a penny on the ground. I walked over it and didn't intend to pick it up because it was *only a penny*. Suddenly, I heard God whisper in my heart: "If you pick up pennies, someday you will be very successful." I instantly knew it wasn't about the penny but the principle of paying attention to little things. For Dave and me, paying attention to little things has been a foundational principle for our lives and ministry for many years. We think little things are important. Our entire family, including our grandchildren, pick up pennies every time we see them. Each penny is a reminder of what God said all those years ago when He was so intensely teaching me to walk in the Spirit. He has caused our ministry to be successful and allowed us to have the great privilege of spreading His Word around the world.

CHAPTER 8

The Mind of the Spirit

The mind governed by the flesh is death, but the mind governed by the Spirit is life and peace.

Romans 8:6 NIV

I wrote about the mind in chapter 4 because dealing with the question "What do I think?" is so important to leaving behind selfish living and embracing the joy that comes from thinking of others. The mind is vital to our walk with God and to living the good life He desires for us, so I want to address it more in this chapter.

As I have mentioned, during the years I suffered incest and sexual abuse, I made a vow to myself that once I got away from home, I would never depend on anyone but myself. Since I had grown up never getting what I wanted because the people around me used me instead of loving me, I determined that I would get what I wanted from that time forward. My view of life was rooted in fear, shame, guilt, and other negative emotions that made me feel bad about myself. My thoughts fed my feelings, and this kept me self-focused and unhappy.

At that time, I had no idea that I could change my life by changing my thoughts. I didn't know I could change my thinking by casting down one thought and choosing another. I spent years thinking whatever thoughts came to my mind, most of which were planted by the devil and consisted of destructive lies, deceiving me and leading me in wrong directions.

> Bad thoughts produce bad feelings.

Anytime you are unhappy, just think about what you are thinking about, and you will probably locate the reason for your lack of joy. Bad thoughts produce bad feelings.

After I became a Christian, I had to learn that I have the mind of Christ (1 Corinthians 2:16). As I mentioned earlier, this means we have the ability to think as He does, and we can choose and learn to do so. We have the mind of Christ; we simply have to develop it and form the habit of choosing godly thoughts. When we want to align our thoughts with His, the Holy Spirit will always help us do it.

No matter what situation you are in, ask yourself, "What would Jesus think under these circumstances?" Then think accordingly. Most people have the mistaken idea that they cannot control their thinking, but you can think thoughts on purpose. I refer to the godly thoughts we deliberately choose to think as "power thoughts." In fact, I have written a book called *Power Thoughts*, and it is designed to help you become firmly established in thinking the thoughts God would have you think.

You can spend time each morning thinking thoughts that will add power to your life and help you be the person God wants you to be, not one who is selfish and self-centered. If you want to become a generous person instead of a selfish one, you must realize that your thinking is the forerunner to any change in your life. Where the mind goes, the man follows. Spend some time in the morning thinking about what you might do for someone else that day, and God will give you some ideas. If we think only about what we want and what others should be doing for us and are not doing for us, we will never overcome being selfish. To be unselfish, we need to think unselfish thoughts.

Set Your Mind

Colossians 3:1–3 says, "Since, then, you have been raised with Christ, set your hearts on things above, where Christ is, seated at the right hand of God. *Set your minds on things above, not on earthly things.* For you died, and your life is now hidden with Christ in God" (NIV, emphasis mine). When this scripture says we should keep our "minds on things above," I don't think it means to think all day long about heaven and what it is like, but to keep our minds on what is wholesome, good, and godly. We should fill our minds with thoughts that God approves of and keep our minds set on things that will benefit us, help others, and honor God.

We need to set our minds on the things of God because whatever we set our minds on, we will go after. In order to walk in the Spirit, we must operate out of the mind of the Spirit, not the mind of the flesh. The amplification of Romans 8:6 describes the mind of the flesh as "sense and reason without the Holy Spirit." I use sense and reason, but I do so with the Holy Spirit's direction and my knowledge of God's Word. When we receive Jesus as our Lord, we get new abilities, and one of them is that we can learn to think differently. According to Romans 8:6, when we think like God thinks, according to the mind of the Spirit, we will enjoy life and peace. We will also have what God wants us to have and be who He wants us to be.

A New Attitude in Your Mind

You were taught, with regard to your former way of life, to put off your old self, which is being corrupted by its deceitful desires; to be made new in the attitude of your minds; and to put on the new self, created to be like God in true righteousness and holiness.

Ephesians 4:22–24 NIV

The apostle Paul gives us a simple formula to help us stop behaving as though we are not born again and to begin to live as the new creation God has made us. He says to put off the old self (Ephesians 4:22) and to put on the new self (Ephesians 4:24). But how do we do this? Verse 23 has the answer. It says to be made new in the attitude of our minds. In the Amplified Bible, Classic Edition, it reads, "And be constantly renewed in the spirit of your mind [having a fresh mental and spiritual attitude]." If we want to behave differently, we have to think differently.

> If you want to behave differently, you have to think differently.

Renewing the mind or learning to think according to God's Word is foundational to learning to live as the new creation God has created us to be in Jesus. Paul writes in 2 Corinthians 5:17: "Therefore, if anyone is in Christ, he is a new creation; old things have passed away; behold, all things have become new" (NKJV). We might say we get a brand-new beginning.

One of the best things we can do for ourselves is to work with the Holy Spirit to have our mind renewed. Our thinking is extremely important, and believe it or not, we can control our thoughts. We can choose what to think. Think happy and be happy!

When we are born again, we become new, soft spiritual clay for God to remold into His original intention for us, His intention before sin came into the world. This is a process that often takes more time than we thought it would or think it should, and it is more painful than we expect. It requires "crucifying the flesh" or "dying to self." (I will explain these concepts in detail later in the book, but you can probably tell that they are not easy, pleasant experiences, though they eventually lead to great blessings.) Ask God to do what He wants to with you, and ask that He will enable you not to resist Him but to cooperate with Him. I like the phrase *dying to live*. If we will die to self (selfishness, self-will, self-centeredness), then we can finally really live the life Jesus died for us to live.

Before any of this can transpire, we first need to renew our mind by learning to think differently than we did previously. Instead of "What about me?" thoughts, we learn to think of others and how we can be a blessing to them. Because this kind of thinking is opposed to our natural nature, we have to practice thinking properly, and practice takes time, patience, and repetition.

We need to learn to meditate on God's Word, especially in areas that will help us not to be selfish. To meditate means to roll something over and over in your mind. If you know how to worry, then you know how to meditate. Meditation is for our minds like chewing our food is for our bodies. If we swallow our food whole or chew it very little, we don't get all of the nutrition out of it. It is good to read or hear a scripture, but what we really need to do is meditate on the Word in order to get the most out of it.

Mark 4:24 says, "And He said to them, Be careful what you are hearing. The measure [of thought and study] you give [to the truth you hear] will be the measure [of virtue and knowledge] that comes back to you—and more [besides] will be given to you who hear." Hearing or reading a scripture gives you a little knowledge or information, but if you want revelation, more power and understanding, you will need to meditate on it. By doing this you break it down, and you receive revelation that becomes part of you and then enables you to do what it instructs you to do.

In order to break the power of selfishness, I meditated, studied, and confessed (spoke aloud) scriptures on loving God and others and on being generous and giving, on believing the best, on forgiving, being merciful, and not being critical or judgmental. I started doing this forty-five years ago and still do it regularly. I also regularly practice intentionally thinking about what I can do for others. My goal is to do something for someone every day. I haven't reached that goal yet, but I am pressing toward it. I lived many years as a selfish person, and I will do whatever I need to do to not be that way again.

Here are six of these types of scriptures, which you can study, meditate on, and speak aloud:

> Jesus replied: "'Love the Lord your God with all your
> heart and with all your soul and with all your mind.' This

is the first and greatest commandment. And the second is like it: 'Love your neighbor as yourself.' All the Law and the Prophets hang on these two commandments."

Matthew 22:37–40 NIV

Let each of you look not only to his own interests, but also to the interests of others.

Philippians 2:4 ESV

But if anyone has the world's goods and sees his brother in need, yet closes his heart against him, how does God's love abide in him?

1 John 3:17 ESV

Do not neglect to do good and to share what you have, for such sacrifices are pleasing to God.

Hebrews 13:16 ESV

Give, and it will be given to you. Good measure, pressed down, shaken together, running over, will be put into your lap. For with the measure you use it will be measured back to you.

Luke 6:38 ESV

Be kind to one another, tenderhearted, forgiving one another, as God in Christ forgave you.

Ephesians 4:32 ESV

Learning to Want What God Wants

Matthew writes, "From that time Jesus began to show his disciples that he must go to Jerusalem and suffer many things from the elders and chief priests and scribes, and be killed, and on the third day be raised" (Matthew 16:21 ESV). Peter pulled Jesus aside "and began to rebuke him, saying, 'Far be it from you, Lord! This shall never happen to you'" (Matthew 16:22 ESV). At that point, Jesus turned and said to Peter, "Get behind me, Satan! You are a hindrance to me. For you are not setting your mind on the things of God, but on the things of man" (Matthew 16:23 ESV).

In this scenario, Peter seems to have been thinking selfishly. We know he cared for Jesus, but I believe He also was concerned that, since He was one of His disciples, if Jesus suffered, he might also suffer. Perhaps some of his concern was rooted in a selfish motive.

Later on, Jesus prayed throughout the night in the Garden of Gethsemane, asking God to remove the cup of suffering from Him if possible. Every time He asked God to spare Him the suffering that awaited Him, He followed the request with "nevertheless, not as I will, but as you will" (Matthew 26:39 ESV) and "your will be done" (Matthew 26:42 ESV). In Matthew 26:44 (ESV), we read that He "prayed for the third time, saying the same words again."

Jesus had asked the disciples to pray with Him for just one hour, but they all fell asleep. Since He asked the Father three separate times for the cup of suffering to be removed, He obviously didn't want to go to the cross and suffer a horrible death, but He was willing to do whatever God wanted no matter how hard it was. He had set His mind to do the will of God! Have you done that? Jesus wanted what His Father wanted more than He wanted what He Himself wanted, and we should feel the same way.

Changed by Renewing the Mind

According to Romans 12:2, we are changed by the entire renewal of the mind. I cannot stress how important this one biblical truth is. Our thoughts become our words, our attitudes, and our actions (behavior). We absolutely cannot change our behavior until we change our mind. This scripture teaches us that if we want to see God's good plan fulfilled in our life, we have to completely renew the mind. God's Word is the tool that He uses to accomplish this. God's thoughts and His words are one and the same. Learn the Word, and you will learn to think as God does.

For as long as we live before we accept Jesus as our Savior, our thinking is worldly and operates according to the flesh. It is selfish and self-centered, and the question "What about me?" goes through our thoughts frequently. We want to make sure we are taken care of and that we get what we want, even if it means others do not get what they want. Selfish people are not concerned with the interests of others. They are concerned only with their own interests, desires, wants, and needs, and they spend their time trying to obtain them. All their thoughts are selfish.

Our old selves are not dead, but we are instructed to die to sin and to our old ways. Charles Spurgeon wrote, "It is at once the most Christlike and the most happy course for a believer to cease from living to himself."[9] It is amazing how happy we are when we stop living a selfish and self-centered life, and to get the full impact of it, we must experience it for ourselves. The devil ferociously resists us in our attempt to die to self and live wholly for God and serve others. But remaining firm in our determination to die to self with God's help will eventually produce success.

I will elaborate on the idea of dying to self later in the book, but here let me simply say that dying to self means that although you have a will that wants to follow its desires, a mind that wants to think your own thoughts, and emotions that want you to let them lead you, you can say no to all these and choose to live God's way. Each time you do, a little

> *Dying to self means choosing to live God's way.*

more of your flesh loses control over you, and eventually it will not control you at all. But, in the spirit of fairness, I need to tell you that the journey may not be a short one. It often requires the Holy Spirit dealing with us several—or many—times about the same thing before we finally always let God take the lead.

We Want to Know

The mind of the Spirit, as you can see in this chapter, is not like the mind of the flesh. In our human minds, the quest for knowledge is huge, but when we have the mind of the Spirit, we are content to know what God wants us to know. Although we do want to learn what we need to know and be informed about what is going on, we can become so entrenched in the desire to find reasons for everything that happens that we become crippled mentally and spiritually. I have said that at one time in my life I was addicted to reasoning, meaning I thought and thought about everything, trying to understand it with my natural mind. I could not calm down unless I thought I had everything figured out. I often felt what turned out to be false peace because I thought I had certain answers, only to find out later that what I thought was actually incorrect. It is interesting that I felt calm and peaceful, even though what I thought was wrong. That's how driven I was to figure things out and how important having an answer was to me. This was the result of being determined to take care of myself and not need anyone else.

I am so glad I've finally been delivered from the need to know everything and the pressure to think so much. We can make ourselves miserable by overthinking things. I do still ask God questions, but I'm no longer bothered if He doesn't give me answers. Sometimes the answer is that I don't need to know; I simply need to trust Him.

Prior to his conversion, Paul sought knowledge. He was highly educated, but he reached the point where he decided to know nothing except Jesus Christ and Him crucified (1 Corinthians 2:2). He also said that He wanted to know Him and the power of His resurrection (Philippians 3:10 NIV). I would think this simplified his life greatly. Excessive reasoning or overthinking can be tiring and confusing. It causes frustration, but simple trust in God brings peace.

James 1:22 indicates that we can betray ourselves "into deception by reasoning contrary to the Truth." This prevents us from obeying God's Word. When God asks us to do something we don't want to do, our flesh can fabricate endless excuses. We can always find reasons to disobey God, but they are reasons contrary to the truth of His Word. Excuses are dangerous because they give us permission to do what is wrong and deceive ourselves into thinking it is right.

Taking personal responsibility instead of offering excuses is vital to our spiritual maturity. The longer we blame other people for our wrong behaviors, the longer we will stay in bondage to them. Make a decision to stop making excuses. Ask the Holy Spirit to help you, and even if someone else did cause the problems you have, you are the only one who can take responsibility to begin doing what will get you out of trouble and into spiritual health and maturity.

> *Taking personal responsibility is vital to your spiritual maturity.*

CHAPTER 9

The Natural and the Spiritual

The natural person does not accept the things of the Spirit of God, for they are folly to him, and he is not able to understand them because they are spiritually discerned. The spiritual person judges all things, but is himself to be judged by no one.

1 Corinthians 2:14–15 ESV

The natural (nonspiritual) person doesn't understand the spiritual person because the things of the Spirit can only be spiritually discerned. A good example of this happened to me several years ago when an accountant was helping me with my taxes. He told me I was giving too much money to the church. He did not understand God's principle of sowing and reaping (Galatians 6:7–8). It made no sense to him. But because I have studied God's Word and endeavor to obey it in every way, giving money to support God's work made perfect sense to me.

People who have not been taught God's Word tend to look at life through the lens of sense and reasoning. If certain things don't make sense to their minds, they don't believe them. If I looked at God's Word with only my natural mind, much of it would not make sense to me, either. For example, why should I give away some of what I have in order to gain more (2 Corinthians 9:6–8)? How can the first be last and the last be first (Matthew 20:16)? Why should I love, bless, pray for, and forgive my enemies (Luke 6:27–28; Mark 11:25)? The Bible teaches us to do these things, but people who don't know God tend to reject doing them because they don't seem logical. If we set our minds to be obedient to God, we must do so with a heart of faith, not merely a head full of natural knowledge. People who are spiritual believe what they cannot see or feel (Hebrews 11:1); they believe in their hearts. I didn't see Jesus die on the cross, but I wholeheartedly believe He did and that He did it for you and me. People who are spiritual believe the Word of God regardless of

> People who have not been taught God's Word look at life through the lens of sense and reasoning.

what they see or do not see, but those who are natural only believe what they see with their eyes.

In Luke 5:1–11, we read that several men who would become Jesus' disciples had fished all night and caught nothing. They were washing their nets and closing up shop for the day. They had worked hard and were tired and disappointed because they had caught no fish. Jesus appeared to them and told them to launch out into the deep, where they would catch a lot of fish. Peter said, "Master, we toiled all night [exhaustingly] and caught nothing [in our nets]. But on the ground of Your word, I will lower the nets [again]" (v. 5). When he did, they pulled in a huge catch (v. 6), so many fish that their boats began to sink, and they had to call for their partners in boats nearby to help them (v. 7). Peter trusted what Jesus said more than what made sense to his natural mind. He was very tired and didn't want to fish anymore that day. He didn't think it would work and didn't feel like doing it, but he did it based solely on Jesus' word. This is the attitude God wants us to have toward what He instructs us to do.

Hearing from God

Everyone can hear from God. As we walk in the Spirit, we learn to hear His voice as He leads us and helps us. But people who are too logical often have difficulty hearing from Him because much of what God wants us to do doesn't make sense to our logical or fleshly mind. We must be extra careful when trying to hear from God about something we strongly want to do. Does God approve of our doing it, or is it just something we would like to do? Suppose you want a new car, but you really cannot afford to buy one. You will have to go into deeper

> *Everyone can hear from God.*

debt than you are already in, and you know the purchase isn't a wise choice. But you *really* want the car. You don't even bother to pray about it because you already know in your heart what the answer will be. God won't stop loving you if you buy the car, and you won't lose your salvation if you buy it. But you will be under the pressure of more debt, and before long, you'll wish you hadn't bought the car, because once the shiny newness wears off, it won't be much different from the one you had before, except the payment will be larger.

We must be careful about our emotions when it comes to situations like this. Just because we feel something doesn't mean the feelings are from God. Just this week I started planning something I wanted to do, but after praying about it, I realized it wasn't wise. What we need is spiritual discernment, not head knowledge, ego, logic, or emotion. We also need to pray about decisions and give God an opportunity to speak to us about our choices. Doing this is respectful to the Lord and honors Him.

One of our daughters has two dogs, and I recall what she went through when they were puppies. She has twin daughters, and they wanted twin dogs, so they have two Maltese that are sisters. Recently, my daughter and her husband went to a pet store and saw another darling baby Maltese. She called me and sent me pictures, and I could hear her on the phone pleading with her husband to let her have the puppy. She was very emotional. Her husband told her he absolutely did not want another dog, and they went home with no puppy. When she woke up the next morning, she thought, *Thank God I didn't buy that puppy!* It is amazing how much trouble a good night's sleep can keep us out of. Before making a major decision, try sleeping on it and see if you feel the same the next morning as you did the night before.

> Do what God tells you to do, not whatever you feel like doing.

God wants us to do what He tells us to do,

not just whatever we feel like doing. If we don't follow His leading, there are consequences. Those consequences are not God punishing us; they are the natural results of wrong choices. If we spend more money than we have, we will bear the consequence of being in debt, which causes stress, often marital problems, and even sickness, in the case of long-term stress.

You might ask, "What about forgiveness?" If we are repentant, God does forgive us and sometimes even gives us mercy that lessens or removes the consequences. But if we keep having to learn the same lesson over and over, God will finally let us have the consequences to help us learn not to do it again. If this happens, it is always and only done in love. God chastens (corrects and disciplines) those He loves (Hebrews 12:6 NKJV).

When it comes to hearing from God, we all make mistakes at times. A wonderful, mature man of God was asked how he learned to hear from God, and he said, "By making a lot of mistakes." Don't be so afraid of making a mistake that you won't venture out into learning how to hear from God, and how to be led by discernment instead of by your natural mind. No toddler ever learns how to walk without falling down many times. If you misunderstand what God is saying and make a mistake, He will find you and help you get back on the right track.

Discernment

What is discernment? *To discern* simply means to distinguish between good and evil. Proverbs talks about this at length. Discernment is viewed as a virtue in the Christian faith. A discerning person is considered to have wisdom and be of good judgment.

> A discerning person has wisdom and exercises good judgment.

This chapter's opening scripture tells us that the spiritual person discerns, while the natural person cannot do that. Discernment comes from a person's spirit (inmost being). By discernment, we know what is right or wrong, good or evil. One of the gifts of the Spirit that Paul mentions in 1 Corinthians 12 is the gift of discerning spirits (v. 10). People who have this gift know the nature of the spirit in or on a person. If they are around someone evil, they will recognize it. They will also know if the person has good intentions and whether or not getting involved with them would be wise. They may have no natural proof, but they know in their spirit and are wise enough to listen to that discernment over and above what they see, think, or feel.

Because there is so much deception in our world today, discernment is more important than ever. But please remember that people who are natural don't have spiritual discernment because they judge based on natural knowledge, logic, and what is visible to the natural eye.

There have been times when someone has applied for a position with our ministry and, on paper, that person seemed well qualified. Everything looked great, but I just did not feel good about them in my spirit. Anytime I have ignored that inner sense of caution, it has always caused trouble. But when I have heeded it, life remains peaceful. The amplification of Colossians 3:15 teaches us to let peace "act as umpire" in our lives. Umpires say what is in or out in sports games, and if we let peace be our umpire, it will let us know when we should or should not do something.

> Let peace be your umpire.

Our youngest son has a strong gift of discernment and wisdom far beyond his years and experience. He is the CEO of all media and operations for our ministry and does a wonderful job, largely because he has discernment about what to do and what not to do. He can discern when the right time is for certain things and when we should wait. He takes his time making decisions. He lets things sit in his heart for a while to see if what he senses is right. I can't even count all the times he has told me that such-and-such a person is not someone we want to be involved with or that someone is doing something they shouldn't be doing. Looking at the person with my natural eye, I didn't see a problem at all, but later on my son turned out to be right. Discernment is a wonderful ability to have. Not everyone has the spiritual gift of discernment, but we can all develop more of it by learning to listen to our heart, being more intuitive, and making sure we have peace about our decisions.

Always pray about the decisions you make. You may feel one way about a certain choice before you pray about it, and you may feel differently after you pray. Acknowledge God in all you do, and you are more likely to be led by the Spirit. Just today, I was all excited about doing something. I wanted to go to Brazil and minister the Word, but I had not prayed about it yet. After I started praying, I saw all kinds of reasons such a trip would not be a good idea for me at this time. Let me say again: *Always pray about important decisions before making them.* I also recommend that when you make major decisions, you wait before giving a final answer. Whether it is one night or a few days, waiting a little while is much better than making an irreversible mistake that will cause heartache or difficulty, perhaps for years.

Being in a rush to get what we want can be a symptom of selfishness. After all, whatever it is, we want it. We think we deserve it. We are going to get it! However, if we do something simply out of self-centeredness and don't use wisdom, we will not be happy in the long term—no matter how much we get. We may be happy temporarily because we got what we wanted, but reality will set in eventually and sorrow will drown out any happiness we may have felt. Right this moment, I imagine thousands upon thousands of people are miserable because of an emotional decision they made that could have been avoided had they simply been patient and taken time to ask God to help them discern what to do.

Emotions Fluctuate

While it is a mistake to make decisions based on logic alone, it's also a huge mistake to make decisions based on emotions alone. Emotions fluctuate constantly. They go up and down like a yo-yo. We may agree to do something or purchase something when emotions are high, and when they settle down to a normal level, we regret what we did. I often say, "Let emotions subside and then decide," especially if the decision you are making is a big one. Don't make decisions when emotions are running high or when they are sunken and low.

> Let emotions subside,
> then decide.

I have been on sixty-seven international mission trips, and many of them included forty-plus hours of flying round trip and a heavy work schedule while overseas. We hosted crusades in these countries, and on the last night of each one, the crowds were often huge. The attendance at a specific crusade I remember was more than one million people over the four evenings we were there. In the midst of the amazing worship music, getting to preach to that many people, and seeing hundreds of thousands receive Christ, I got very excited. After experiences such as these, I recall a number of times getting on the plane to return home and talking to our oldest son, who is the CEO of Hand of Hope, Joyce Meyer Ministries World Missions, about starting to plan another trip to the same place the next year. Based on our conversation, he would start making plans. After I got home and was super tired and dealing with jet lag, I often called him and said, "Why don't we wait on planning another trip to that location right now since we have so many others to do?" After this happened several times, he learned that he needed to wait until my emotions calmed down before he started planning return trips.

When I am rested and feel strong, I think I can do anything. But my family and leadership team have realized now that I am not as young as I once was and that what I *think* I can do and what I can *actually* do are two different things. My family steps in and says, "*No, Mom.* You cannot do that; it is too hard on you. You don't need to travel any more than you already do."

Thankfully, I can reach more people in thirty minutes on television than I can running around the globe trying to teach people in person. Being in the television studio may not be as exciting for me as traveling to foreign countries, but it will help me live longer and bear more fruit in the long run. It is important for all of us to do what will bear the most fruit for God's kingdom instead of merely doing what is exciting. Excitement is short lived, but peace is enduring, and it is one of the most valuable resources we can have.

> Excitement is short lived, but peace is enduring.

Remember, natural people live by what they want, think, and feel. But those who are spiritual live by discernment and by God's Word. When you need to make a decision, talk to God about it and quiet your soul (your mind, will, and emotions) so you can discern what He is leading you to do.

CHAPTER 10

Dying to Self

Then he said to them all: "Whoever wants to be my disciple must deny themselves and take up their cross daily and follow me."

Luke 9:23 NIV

In this chapter of the book and the two following it, I pray that I'm able to explain to you more clearly what dying to self and crucifying the flesh (sin nature) require. The key chapters in the New Testament that help us understand dying to self and help empower us to do it are Romans 6–8.

Thus far in the book, I have mentioned what I believe to be the three components of selfishness: following what we want, think, and feel without caring how it affects others. Hopefully you now see how focusing on what we want, think, and feel combine to make for a very selfish life. These are functions of the soul (flesh), meaning they emanate from our natural human nature. They all have one word in common: *I*, which refers to the self. Remember, people who are selfish live their lives with three questions in mind: "What do *I* want?" "What do *I* think?" "How do *I* feel?" And they often think or say, "What about me?"

The Spirit and the Word Help
Us Die to Self

When I reached the point in my life where I knew I needed to die to self (following my own will) and crucify my flesh, instead of working with the Holy Spirit and learning to consider myself to have died with Christ as Romans 6:8 says, I kept feeding my flesh. This, of course, kept it very much alive. To put the flesh to death simply means to stop letting it control you. This is not something anyone can do by willpower alone. We must have the Holy Spirit strengthening and helping us constantly, which He is ever ready to do if we will ask Him to and cooperate with Him. "Dying to self" is another way of saying growing into spiritual maturity or being transformed into the image of Christ (Romans 8:29).

Our flesh tells us what we want, what we think, and what we feel, but it doesn't tell us what God's will is. To know God's will, we must know God's Word and learn to listen to the Holy Spirit.

Speaking of the flesh, Paul writes that we died when Christ died (Romans 6:6–8). Yet he also says that we must think of ourselves as dead to sin but alive to God in Christ (Romans 6:11). Do you see yourself as Christ says you are? Or do you see yourself according to the way you behave? Your behavior will not change until your beliefs about yourself change. This principle can be confusing, so I'll try to explain it simply.

> Your behavior will not change until your beliefs about yourself change.

We don't always feel that we experience being dead to sin, so we don't believe we are dead to it. So, we keep trying to die to what the Bible says we are already dead to. In the natural realm, we want to see and feel things before we believe them, but in God's kingdom, it is the opposite. We must believe by faith what God's Word says before we see it happen. Faith is the evidence and proof of the reality of things unseen (Hebrews 11:1). We should believe we are dead to sin and that it has no power over us, and then we will begin to live in victory over sin. We learn to believe the things of God by having our mind renewed. As I began to learn the power of right thinking, I starting thinking on purpose, *I am dead to sin*. This intentional thought helped me to finally believe this biblical truth. We must learn to believe God's Word more than we believe what we experience. We will never be entirely without sin, but we can sin less and less as we learn who we are in Christ and truly understand what He has done for us.

> Believe God's Word more than you believe what you experience.

Remember the Israelites

Remember the Israelites, who were held in bondage in Egypt. When they came out of Egypt, a place of bondage, Egypt was still in them, meaning that they still had the mentality that comes with captivity. Several times when their circumstances were difficult, they wanted to return to Egypt. Why would they want to go back into slavery and bondage instead of pressing through the difficulties in order to reach freedom? Because people tend to default to what they are familiar with when life is challenging. For example, a former drug addict may want to run back to drugs when life is difficult, or an alcoholic may want to run for alcohol when life is hard. This is why new believers often are tempted to return to their old lifestyle when they discover that their new life in Christ is not always easy.

Even though most of the people who left Egypt died in the wilderness, with the exception of Joshua and Caleb (Numbers 32:11–13), their children entered the Promised Land, known as Canaan. They still had much to learn, and God taught them to trust Him as they saw His faithfulness time and time again.

Just as the Israelites had to learn to live in the freedom they had been given, we have to learn to live in the freedom from sin that Christ has given us. When we are born again, we are given a new nature, and although our old self legally died with Christ when He died, we still have to remind ourselves frequently that the old nature is dead and not let it control us.

Study and Understand

It is very important for us to study and understand Romans 6–8, because in these chapters Paul presents thoroughly the doctrine of being dead to sin. A Bible commentary can be helpful in understanding them, and many good ones are available, such as ones written by Matthew Henry, Warren Wiersbe, D. L. Moody, and Charles Spurgeon. Martyn Lloyd-Jones also has a wonderful study on the entire Book of Romans. Understanding often requires deep study, and the subject of being dead to sin is one that I believe does require study before you will have the revelation needed in these areas. Simply reading this book will not be enough. They are not areas that are taught frequently, but I believe they are some of the most important ones in the Bible.

CHAPTER 11

Living to God

I have been crucified with Christ [in Him I have shared His crucifixion]; it is no longer I who live, but Christ (the Messiah) lives in me; and the life I now live in the body I live by faith in (by adherence to and reliance on and complete trust in) the Son of God, Who loved me and gave Himself up for me.

Galatians 2:20

Determining exactly when certain events happened in the ancient world can be difficult, and scholars sometimes disagree. But my research indicates that Paul wrote his epistle to the Galatians about AD 55–59, after having converted to Christ in AD 33. This means he wrote that it was no longer he who lived, but Christ who lived in him, twenty-two to twenty-five years after his initial encounter with Jesus (Acts 9). This is encouraging to me, because to be able to say and really mean "It is no longer I who live, but Christ (the Messiah) lives in me" takes time and experience with God. We must die to self in order to live to God, but this process can be painful in our soul at times. We are making progress all the time, but completely dying to self means letting go of things we don't want to relinquish and may think we cannot let go of. But remember that God never tries to take something you like away from you in order to be mean or to punish you. He always guides you to do what will benefit you in the long run because He loves you and only wants the best for you. Once we truly believe this, it is much easier to let go quickly.

Paul writes that we are dead to sin, but not that sin is dead (Romans 6:11 NIV). Sin is very much alive, and the temptation to sin is part of our lives. But in Christ we are dead to sin, meaning that because God gives us a new nature when we are born again, we really don't want to sin. We may often feel that part of us wants to sin, and part of us wants to be holy and do everything God wants us to do. This is when we can choose not to sin.

There is no point in praying we won't be tempted, because we will all be tempted at various times and in various ways. Jesus says in Luke 17:1 that "Temptations . . . are sure to come." Instead, we should pray that we won't succumb to the temptation. The

Lord's Prayer says, "Lead us not into temptation" (Matthew 6:13 NIV). It does not say "remove temptation from us."

The devil can *tempt* us to sin, but he cannot *force* us to sin. We are to resist sin in the power of the Holy Spirit—and the sooner we do, the easier the temptation is to overcome. Jesus even says, "If your right eye causes you to sin, tear it out and throw it away...And if your right hand causes you to sin, cut it off and throw it away" (Matthew 5:29–30 ESV). He doesn't want us to literally pull out our eye and cut off our hand; He is giving us a word picture of how decisively and aggressively we need to deal with sin.

> The devil can tempt you to sin, but he cannot force you to sin.

For example, if you are a married woman working with a man you are attracted to and he flirts with you regularly and invites you to lunch or even plainly asks you to go out with him, tell him no firmly. If his flirtation continues and you can feel yourself weakening and think you may give in, find another job. The same principle applies to a married man who is tempted to sin by having an affair with a woman who is not his wife. If you cannot resist a specific temptation, *get away from it*. We should run from temptation like we would run from a poisonous snake.

Likewise, if you are trying to lose weight and cannot resist sweets, don't have them in your home. If you need to buy them for your family, then throw away the leftovers after your family members have had what they wanted. A friend recently told me, "I bought a quart of ice cream and ate a reasonable portion. Then I threw away the rest because I knew I would eat it if I kept it."

I have formed a habit that helps me not to overeat. I eat until I first start feeling full. Then I push my plate away from me. If I am eating out, as soon as I see the server, I ask them to remove my plate. If anyone is eating with me and wants to take home what's left, I ask for a to-go box. If I leave the food sitting there, I might be tempted to take one more bite, then one more, and then one more until I end up feeling uncomfortable because I have eaten too much.

Stop Thinking about It

We become what we think about in our hearts (Proverbs 23:7). This is why it's so important to stop thinking about the sin that is tempting you. Thinking about it, yet hoping you won't do it, is flirting with sin. A person can commit adultery in their mind, according to Matthew 5:28. God wants us to be pure in heart, which means to have pure thoughts.

> But clothe yourself with the Lord Jesus Christ (the Messiah), and make no provision for [indulging] the flesh [put a stop to thinking about the evil cravings of your physical nature] to [gratify its] desires (lusts).
>
> Romans 13:14

You won't do something you never imagine (think about) yourself doing. To die to self means to choose to do God's will instead of what we want, think, or feel—no matter how difficult it is. To do this, we need a lot of help from the Holy Spirit, so be sure to ask Him for it. When you begin your journey toward dying to self, it will be very difficult. You may fail many times, as we all do. But if you continue in God's Word and exercise your faith to resist temptation, eventually you will become, as Paul writes, "dead to sin" (Romans 6:11). When you do make mistakes, repent, receive God's forgiveness, and let go of them. Don't waste time feeling guilty. Follow Paul's example in Philippians 3:13–14 (NIV):

> Dying to self means choosing to do God's will.

Brothers and sisters, I do not consider myself yet to have taken hold of it. But one thing I do: Forgetting what is behind and straining toward what is ahead, I press on toward the goal to win the prize for which God has called me heavenward in Christ Jesus.

As we die to self, we will experience real pain—not physical pain but emotional pain. Instead of resisting it, I recommend that you relax and let it do its work. When a woman is giving birth, the natural temptation is to resist the pain, but the medical professionals attending her remind her to relax and breathe into it. Dying to self is much like giving birth. You are giving birth to a new you, a you who is more concerned with God's will than with your own.

> As you die to self, you will experience emotional pain.

No one enjoys not getting their way, but following God's will is always better in the long run. In the process of giving up what we want, we don't realize that God's way will be better than what we currently have. The longer we are on the journey of dying to self, the more we do realize that God's way is better, even if we don't understand it at the time.

The less you think about your own way, the easier it will be to let it go. Our thoughts affect us more than anything else, and yours can be your keys to victory. When you are tempted to sin, think about what giving in to that sin will produce. Don't think only about the moment of pleasure you expect to get from doing it; think of the consequences.

If you were an alcoholic and have been sober for two years, the last thing you should do is hang out with your friends at a bar. If you do need to be somewhere liquor is being served and are tempted to drink it, just remember what your life was like before you got sober. Then ask yourself if you really want to go back to that situation.

There are times when I am tempted to do something I know I should not do or behave in a way that I know would not please God, and I talk to myself aloud. I say, "Joyce, stop it. Do what you know you should do, not what you feel like doing." This always helps me.

Selfishness Leads to a Lonely Life

Selfish people end up lonely people.

People who are selfish end up lonely. Jesus says in John 12:24, "I assure you, most solemnly I tell you, Unless a grain of wheat falls into the earth and dies, it remains [just one grain; it never becomes more but lives] by itself alone. But if it dies, it produces many others and yields a rich harvest."

Jesus died, rose from the dead, and was the firstborn among many (Romans 8:29). He had to die to open the way for us to follow. He died so we could live, and we must die to self (selfishness) so we can be a good example to others and so they can find Christ and experience true life in Him. I have had the privilege of teaching millions of people over the years, but had I refused to die to self, I would have missed the joy of being able to help those people. I'm sure God would have found someone who would obey Him, but I would have missed the greatest privilege of my life. I still make mistakes, as we all do. But my goal is to not be selfish and self-centered, and I believe I am making progress toward it little by little.

Give yourself away and live for what God desires.

The key to true happiness is to give yourself away and live for what God desires.

Lonely in a Crowd

People who are self-centered can be lonely even in a room filled with others. They are focused on themselves, so all they have is themselves. They dwell on how they look and what people think of them. They wonder how other people like the clothes they are wearing or their hairstyle. If someone who is important in the world's estimation is there, they try to get close to that person so they can feel important also. If no one seems to pay much attention to them, they go home miserable and lonelier than when they arrived. People who are selfish and insecure are sure nobody likes them, and they are being ignored on purpose. This may not be true, but they believe it because they are obsessed with themselves.

As Steve Maraboli says, "Selfish people tend to only be good to themselves... then are surprised when they are alone."[10]

Pride

Pride is the root of all selfishness. Prideful people think about what is happening to them without being sensitive to what is happening to others. God wants us to be humble. True humility doesn't mean thinking of yourself in lowly ways; it means not being consumed with thinking about yourself and how you can get what you want. People who walk in humility

> God wants you to be humble.

humble themselves under God's mighty hand and trust Him to exalt them in due time, according to 1 Peter 5:6. They are happy being a blessing to others. But selfish, proud people only want to be blessed personally. When we are free of pride and selfishness, then and only then can the Holy Spirit fill every aspect of our lives. A good question to ask ourselves is "How often do I think about others compared to how often I think of myself?" If all married people asked themselves each morning, "What can I do for my spouse today?" I doubt there would be many divorces.

> Ask yourself, "What can I do for others today?"

Selfish pride leads to arrogance because it causes us to think we are better than other people. The amplification of Romans 12:3 tells us that we should not have an exaggerated opinion of our own importance, but see ourselves according to the faith God has given us. In other words, if you are good at something, it is because God has enabled you to be so. Those who look down on others who cannot do what they can do are full of pride and erroneously think they have something to do with the abilities they have. When we see ourselves as better than others, we view them as "beneath" us and treat them accordingly. If we pay attention to the president of a corporation but ignore the janitor, we have a problem with pride. If we think we are always right and other people don't know what they are talking about, we have a problem with pride. If we won't listen to others' opinions, we have a problem with pride. If we cannot take correction without becoming angry or defensive, we have a problem with pride. Pride and selfishness work together; where there's one, we also find the other.

Jesus Died So We Could Be
Free from Selfishness

Referring to Jesus, 2 Corinthians 5:15 says, "And he died for all, that those who live should no longer live for themselves but for him who died for them and was raised again" (NIV). I encourage you to look carefully at this verse. Jesus died so we would no longer live for ourselves (selfishly), but so we could live for Him, doing His will. He wants us to enjoy our lives (John 10:10), so surely if we live for Him and others instead of ourselves, we will have more joy. Being unselfish is so important that it is one reason Jesus died for us. He wants us to be free from selfishness. I think the greatest freedom of all is to be free from yourself.

Something that happened to me this morning reminded me of

how relentless selfishness is. In the midst of my writing this book on not being selfish, our daughter called and asked if I would like to eat dinner with them that evening and watch a movie. Dave was out of town, and they were being thoughtful in not wanting me to be alone. They asked what movie I wanted to watch and then made several suggestions. I said no to each one and kept thinking of what *I* wanted to watch. Three hours later, I suddenly realized I was being selfish in not caring which movie they wanted to see as long as I got to watch what I wanted to watch.

This reminded me that selfishness is something we have to be diligent to watch out for and guard against. We must be determined to be "others-minded," not selfish and self-centered. I called my daughter back and told her to choose the movie, because that's what an unselfish person should do. It isn't as though I had in mind a movie I really wanted to watch. I just wanted to be the one to pick the movie to make sure I liked it.

Author Stephen Kendrick says, "Almost every sinful action ever committed can be traced back to a selfish motive. It's a trait we hate in other people but justify in ourselves."[11]

Who Is the Greatest?

They came to Capernaum. When he was in the house, he asked them, "What were you arguing about on the road?" But they kept quiet because on the way they had argued about who was the greatest. Sitting down, Jesus called the Twelve and said, "Anyone who wants to be first must be the very last, and the servant of all."

Mark 9:33–35 NIV

It is encouraging to me to know that even Jesus' disciples were selfish at times, and they argued with one another about who among them was the greatest, as we read in Mark 9:33–35. Pride and ego are our biggest enemies. Humility is a virtue that is not easy to maintain. It must be a matter of special prayer and something we think about regularly. People who are humble don't care if they are first or last, as long as they are in God's will. Remember, if we will humble ourselves, God will exalt us. If we are willing to be last, God often makes us first. But the choice should be His, not something we struggle to attain for ourselves.

Serving others comes naturally to people who have the gift of helping others. I don't have that gift, so I have to serve on purpose. Even if you have the gift of helping others and you love to serve people, you may be selfish in other ways. Selfishness is a disease that afflicts all of us in one way or another.

Charles Spurgeon said, "I have now concentrated all of my prayers into one, and that one prayer is this, that I may die to self, and live wholly to Him."[12] This is an awesome prayer and one we should all pray.

What Are You Full Of?

Paul prays the following prayer for his readers:

> [That you may really come] to know [practically, through experience for yourselves] the love of Christ, which far surpasses mere knowledge [without experience]; that you may be filled [through all your being] unto all the fullness of God [may have the richest measure of the divine Presence, and become *a body wholly filled and flooded with God Himself*]!
>
> Ephesians 3:19 (emphasis mine)

I used to pray regularly that I would simply be a body wholly filled with God, but as I read this Scripture passage to include it in this book, it reminds me that I haven't prayed this prayer in a long while—I will definitely start again. I really don't want to be selfish, and even though I have made progress, I know I have a long way to go.

I spent many years becoming angry when I didn't get my way. Thankfully, I no longer respond with anger when I don't get what I want, but in some areas, I definitely want what I want and am not shy about trying to get it. A weak area for me involves eating. Where and what I eat for my main meal each day is far too important to me. Because of our lifestyle, Dave and I eat out a lot or order food in (meaning, I don't cook). I don't eat much, so what I do eat I want to *love*. I spend far too much time trying to figure out the perfect meal. Now, I guess after sharing my weakness with you, I must commit to changing. No matter how much time I spend trying to figure out the perfect meal, no matter what I eat, once I'm full, it doesn't seem to make any difference.

Imagine how wonderful it would be to simply be someone wholly filled with God. Mark Batterson says: "If you aren't hungry for God, you are full of yourself."[13] Start paying attention to how much you think about yourself and how much energy you expend trying to get your way. Once you know where you are currently, you can begin to improve.

Stay Out of Strife

As we consider what we want for ourselves, we should seek to be led by the Holy Spirit. We should not simply decide we won't want anything for ourselves. As I stated previously, this would be out of balance. One thing is certain, however: We should not allow strife in our relationships as we try to get our way. If we delight ourselves in God, He will give us the desires of our heart (Psalm 37:4), and we won't have to waste our time try-

Trust your desires to God.

ing to make things happen. Trust your desires to God, and let Him give them to you if and when He sees the time is right.

James writes that the things that we want and try to get for ourselves cause strife. And if we cannot get them, then we fight and become jealous, and our desires go unfulfilled (James 4:1). This verse makes clear that we must not allow strife in our relationships as we try to get our way. Instead, we are to simply ask God for what we need. In the next verse, James teaches what I have mentioned several times in this book, "You do not have because you do not ask" (James 4:2 NKJV). Learning this scripture for the first time was a wow moment in my walk with God. I realized that when I wanted something and wasn't getting it, I should pray about it instead of starting strife about it or becoming frustrated as I tried to make it happen in my own strength. If God wanted me to have it, He would get it to me His way and in His timing. This took tremendous pressure off of me.

Dying to self and living to God isn't easy, but it is much better than remaining selfish and self-centered. It may be a lifetime quest, but it is one thing that is worth pursuing.

CHAPTER 12
Belonging to Christ

Those who belong to Christ Jesus have crucified the flesh with its passions and desires.

Galatians 5:24 NIV

The way to belong to Christ is to crucify the flesh (Galatians 5:24). As I noted earlier, when the Bible mentions the flesh, it refers to our sin nature, which is expressed through our bodies, our minds, our wills, and our emotions. When we are born again, we are united with Christ (Philippians 2:1 NIV). Positionally (as a spiritual reality), we become one with Him (John 17:21). And we also become His home because He comes to dwell in us (1 Corinthians 6:19). But God cannot be anywhere that is not holy because He is holy (1 Peter 1:15), so when we are born again, we are made holy and righteous through the blood of Jesus (2 Corinthians 5:21; Hebrews 10:10). Paul also writes in Philemon 6, "That the sharing of your faith may become effective by the acknowledgment of every good thing which is in you in Christ Jesus" (NKJV). When we are in Christ, we are full of good things, and we need to know and acknowledge this.

The work God does in us initially takes place in our spirit and as we work with the Holy Spirit and surrender our mind, will, and emotions to Him, He is able to move into our soul, as well as our spirit. Paul prays for believers in Ephesians 3:16, "May He grant you out of the rich treasury of His glory to be strengthened and reinforced with mighty power in the inner man by the [Holy] Spirit [Himself indwelling your innermost being and personality]" (Ephesians 3:16, emphasis mine).

As we give the Holy Spirit access to our soul, His fruit can be seen through our behavior—and that is the goal. I may have many good things in my spirit, but if they cannot be seen through my soul and in my behavior, I won't be a good witness or example to anyone.

Because you are in Christ, having received Him as your Lord

and Savior, God views you as righteous, holy, a new creation, powerful, strong, wise, unselfish, generous, joyful, peaceful, and every other spiritually good thing you can think of. These attributes are given by God's grace and received through faith in Jesus Christ. They are in your spirit in seed form when you are born again, but they need to be cultivated and grow so they can be expressed through your soul and your flesh. This requires a process that is often long, arduous, and painful.

George Müller made this statement:

> There was a day when I died, utterly died; died to George Müller, his opinions, preferences, tastes and will— died to the world, its approval or censure—died to the approval or blame even of my brethren and friends— and since then I have studied only to show myself approved unto God.[14]

I believe this was the day he decided to live an unselfish life, but I'm sure the journey took time, commitment, determination, and much prayer—as it does for you and me. Nothing happens without a decision, so I encourage you to make the decision to live unselfishly and let God take over from there. Living unselfishly begins with a decision and then requires many subsequent decisions and a great deal of help from the Holy Spirit. I often am being selfish without even realizing it, so I have to ask the Holy Spirit to make me aware when I am behaving selfishly.

When we receive Jesus as Savior and Lord, we have not necessarily surrendered ourselves to Him yet. Positionally, we are "in Christ" and we are seated in heavenly places in Him (Ephesians 2:6). But experientially, we are working with the Holy Spirit to work out of us what Christ has put in us freely by His grace. Jesus can be our Savior without being our Lord. When He is Lord, we

Work with the Holy Spirit to work out of you what Christ has put in.

choose His will instead of our own. When Jesus is Lord, one thing we can never say is "No, Lord." If we say no, then He is not Lord. The only correct answer to any request from God is "Yes, Lord."

This dying to self is a process that takes us finally to the end of ourselves—the end of using our own energy to try to get what we want, trying to change ourselves without God, and trying to change other people. It is a full surrender.

We begin our walk with God full of ourselves, and we usually try to do things on our own, in our human strength, energy, and confidence. We fail time and again, and this frustrates us because we feel we are trying to do what is right. We think we are trying to do what we believe God wants us to do. This may go on for years, depending on how strong our self-will is. Jesus says, "Apart from me you can do nothing" (John 15:5 NIV). We read these words and agree with them, yet we continue either trying to do things on our own or trying a half-and-half formula—some of us and some of Jesus. That doesn't work any better than trying to do it all on our own.

I tried to change myself. I tried to make my ministry grow. I tried to do things I wasn't gifted to do. I tried to change other people (Dave, my children, friends, extended family, and others). I tried very hard, but I never surrendered any of it to God. Even though God wants our full surrender, He waits until we reach the end of ourselves and admit we cannot do it before He will help us. We may surrender to God one area at a time, or we may surrender and then take charge once again and have to make another trip around the "mountain of misery" before we surrender once more. We have a tendency to place things on God's altar (give them up) and then go back and get them.

Cooperate with the Holy Spirit

The Holy Spirit was sent to represent Jesus on earth and to act on His behalf once Jesus ascended to heaven (John 14:16, 16:7). The Holy Spirit's ministry is to help us, teach us all truth, lead and guide us, convict and convince us, and help us pray (John 14:26; 16:8, 16:13; Romans 8:14, 26). He advocates for us before the throne of God (Romans 8:26) and comforts us (John 14:16). It is His job to change us, but we do have to cooperate with Him. He will show us what to do and give us the grace to do it, but we must do the doing. The difference between life before we surrender to Him and life afterward is that before we surrender, we have many ideas about what *we* can do to get what we want, and we try to get it on our own. After we surrender, we only do what the Holy Spirit shows us to do, and we totally depend on Him for the grace to do it. We not only read in John 15:5 that apart from Jesus we can do nothing, but we now truly believe it. Also, at this point we enter the rest of God because we believe God and put our trust in Him instead of the works of our flesh.

Jesus suffered when He was crucified, and we will also suffer as we die to self. I know that *suffering* is not a popular word, but it is a Bible word and one we should not ignore. I read that, depending on the translation, more than seventy scriptures use the word *suffer* or a form of it. First Peter 4:1–2 is one of the passages that helps us understand it:

So, since Christ suffered in the flesh for us, for you, arm yourselves with the same thought and purpose [patiently to suffer rather than fail to please God]. For whoever has suffered in the flesh [having the mind of Christ] is done with [intentional] sin [has stopped pleasing himself and the world, and pleases God], so that he can no longer spend the rest of his natural life living by [his] human appetites and desires, but [he lives] for what God wills.

Our flesh does suffer when it doesn't get its own way. It suffers until we give up control and die to self. Once that happens, the pain stops. I had a particularly hard time letting go of control and learning how to submit to authority, especially male authority. Because I had been abused sexually by my father and several other males, I didn't trust men and found it almost impossible to be happy if I got anything other than my own way. Thankfully Dave is a patient man and was very mature spiritually when we married, even though he was only twenty-six years old.

As a young wife, I had many problems, yet I was not aware that I had any problems at all. I thought everything that went wrong was someone else's fault. When the Holy Spirit began to reveal the truth to me about myself, I was shocked. I was difficult to get along with, selfish, self-centered, manipulating, controlling, insecure, negative—and that's just the beginning of the list.

Because I loved God and wanted to do what He wanted me to do, I began the journey of trying to change myself. That didn't work; it only caused more suffering. Only God can change a human being, because true change must be an inside job. God hasn't called us to behavior modification but to transformation. Only He can cause the good things He has put in us to work their way through our soul and finally be evident in our thoughts, words, and actions. When this happens, everyone knows we have changed not because we tell them, but because they can see the change for themselves.

> *Only God can turn a caterpillar into a butterfly.*

Only God can turn a caterpillar into a butterfly, and only God can turn a selfish, self-centered person into one who is generous and works for the good of others, even if it means personal sacrifice. Paul was willing to give up everything he had in order to really know Christ and become more intimately acquainted with Him (Philippians 3:8).

Sacrifice is not something we hear much about these days. Sadly, people prefer messages that will *give* them something, not ones that teach them to *sacrifice* something. Some people become angry and offended if their pastor talks about giving in ways that seem excessive to them. But I think that when people are giving what they should be giving, they won't be offended by teaching on giving.

For years, I went to church regularly but never heard anything that helped me with my practical problems. I learned a lot of doctrine, and it was valuable, but I needed life lessons. I especially needed someone to tell me that being made whole would hurt like crazy. The reason it hurt so bad was that I had to go back and face things I had run away from or stuffed so far down in my soul that they were unable to surface. I was also full of unforgiveness toward the people who had hurt me, and it was poisoning my soul. Simply facing the fact that the problems I had were my responsibility and no one else's was extremely painful. It hurt my pride. I was the way I was because of the sexual abuse I had suffered, but I was also using my past as an excuse to stay the way I was—even though God was willing to heal me. I was filled with self-pity and blame, and God had to deal with me about all the problems in my soul. If you live with a victim mentality, you will always be a victim. Breaking free and dying to self so you can live for God is an option, and God will help you, but you have to choose to do it.

I was brokenhearted and had a wounded soul, but since pain and woundedness were all I had ever known, I didn't realize it was a problem. I had always had to take care of myself, and I think this fed my tendency to be selfish. I was afraid that if I didn't fight for what I wanted, I would never get it. I had to learn that God doesn't operate like people do and that I could trust Him to give me good things.

Jesus came to heal the brokenhearted (Luke 4:18 NKJV), but I didn't know that. I have now been studying God's Word for more than forty-five years, and I would not trade anything for what I now know. I still have much more to learn, but what I have learned has set me free and enabled me to help others who are still living in spiritual darkness.

Character and the Fruit of the Spirit Must Be Developed

Paul told the Corinthian believers they were carnal (worldly), yet they were born again, baptized in the Holy Spirit, and operating in the gifts of the Spirit. How is it possible that they were also carnal? It's because gifts are given, but character and the fruit of the Spirit must be developed in us. This takes time, study of God's Word, prayer, and cooperation with the Holy Spirit. Some people have gifts that can lead to promotion, but they will ultimately fall because they don't have the character needed to keep them there. This often happens with young gifted Christians who are promoted because of their gifts but have not been mentored in developing godly character.

Consider Paul's words from 1 Corinthians 3:1–3:

> However, brethren, I could not talk to you as to spiritual [men], but as to nonspiritual [men of the flesh, in whom the carnal nature predominates], as to mere infants [in the new life] in Christ [unable to talk yet!] I fed you with milk, not solid food, for you were not

yet strong enough [to be ready for it]; but even yet you are not strong enough [to be ready for it], for you are still [unspiritual, having the nature] of the flesh [under the control of ordinary impulses]. For as long as [there are] envying and jealousy and wrangling and factions among you, are you not unspiritual and of the flesh, behaving yourselves after a human standard and like mere (unchanged) men?

Do You Need a Change?

Often, we want our lives to change, but *we* don't want to change. If you want your life to change, let me ask: Are *you* willing to change? If so, God can begin a work in you. The Holy Spirit will begin to deal with you, and you will need to obey His guidance. He may deal with you through God's Word, through another person, or perhaps through a teaching you hear. Or He may deal with you directly by simply making you aware of things you were previously blind to.

> *If you want your life to change, you must be willing to change.*

One of the best personal examples I know pertains to my mouth and the words I spoke. I had no idea that words had power until I learned from Proverbs 18:21 that "Death and life are in the power of the tongue, and they who indulge in it shall eat the fruit of it [for death or life]." Teaching about the mouth seemed to come at me from every angle. My pastor preached it, guest speakers at our church spoke about it, and I went to the bookstore looking for books on a specific topic and instead found several books on the power of words. As God taught me in various ways about how powerful words are, I changed little by little. My mouth still gets me in trouble from time to time, and I have to repent, but I celebrate how far I have come. I finally reached the place where

I felt immediately convicted when I spoke negative words, gos-
siped, told someone's secrets, uttered words of self-pity, or used
my mouth in other ways that did not honor God. And when I did,
I would repent and start over again. I had to study and study and
study in the area of the mouth and the power of words, because
my mind had to be renewed in that area. I still need refresher
courses from time to time, and you will also.

I went through one difficult situation after another as God led
me in dying to self. I would finally gain victory in one area, and
God would let me rest awhile; then we would start on something
else. I was sure that nobody had as many problems as I did, and
you may feel that way, too. But trust me, everyone has issues that
need to be dealt with. I was already teaching God's Word when He
was dealing with me so intensely, but only for twenty-five people
in a weekly Bible study in my home. I didn't teach things I didn't
know anything about, but as God taught me, I taught it in the
Bible study and found out we all have similar problems.

I had a strong desire to do big things for God, but He only
allowed the ministry to grow as I grew. I had taught God's Word
for fifteen years before He put it on our hearts to go on television.
I had taught the Bible study for five years and spent an entire year
doing nothing in ministry while God did a lot in me. Then I went
to work at a church, and I eventually became an associate pastor
for five years. I learned a lot there, and then at God's direction,
we started our ministry. For five years we were on radio and held
meetings in small hotel ballrooms in areas the radio broadcasts
reached. We also held some weekly meetings in and around St.
Louis, Missouri, where we live.

I took every speaking engagement I was offered, and if I ever got
to preach to a crowd of more than a hundred people, I was very
excited. When I look back and remember how hard we worked
during those years and the ones that followed, I wonder how we

are still alive. I was not only dealing with the work of the ministry, but God was changing me personally and dealing with me about something all the time.

Within a few years after we went on television, we had several hundred employees, and I was still learning how to treat people well. When we have problems in our soul, we usually have problems with people. In addition to all of this, Dave and I were trying to learn how to work together and how to work with the two sons and one daughter who helped us in the ministry. Believe me when I say I have experience and can understand just about any problem you might have. But the good news is that God will give you victory over those problems if you are willing to do things His way instead of yours.

Nothing is impossible with God (Matthew 19:26). If He can change me, He can change anyone. But you will have to be willing for it to take longer than you

> Nothing is impossible with God.

expect, ready to give up anything God asks you to surrender, and ready to endure the pain of crucifying the flesh. Changing is like getting a spiritual operation, but please remember that God won't ask you to handle more than you can bear (1 Corinthians 10:13). In addition, you have His promise that all things work together for good to those who love Him and want His will (Romans 8:28).

PART 4

The Unexpected Path to Joy

CHAPTER 13

Declare War on Selfishness

For wherever there is jealousy (envy) and contention (rivalry and selfish ambition), there will also be confusion (unrest, disharmony, rebellion) and all sorts of evil and vile practices.

James 3:16

It is important to note that according to James 3:16, if we allow selfishness to remain in our lives, we are also inviting in confusion "and all sorts of evil and vile practices." Therefore, I say we must declare war on selfishness and, with God's help, learn to not let it reign in our lives.

Our flesh is selfish, and it will always want what it wants. If it doesn't get what it wants, it will display its dissatisfaction through anger, self-pity, rebellion, and other ugly attitudes. Throughout the Bible we see selfish people. Cain and Abel, sons of Adam and Eve, gave offerings to the Lord. God respected the offering He received from Abel but not the one He received from Cain. Cain killed Abel over this, and I believe he killed his brother because of rivalry and selfish ambition (Genesis 4:1–8; 1 John 3:12). Gehazi, the servant of Elisha, greedily and selfishly went to Naaman in secret and asked him for money and two changes of garments, even though Elisha had declined the offer from Naaman. Then Gehazi lied to Elisha about it. The result was that the leprosy from which Naaman was healed came upon him (2 Kings 5:20–27). He proved with his actions that he could not be trusted.

Even Jesus' disciples were selfish. Selfishness and greed caused Judas to betray Jesus for thirty pieces of silver (Matthew 26:15). The disciples displayed selfishness by competing with one another to see which of them was the greatest (Luke 9:46). In Acts 5:1–4, Ananias and Sapphira selfishly held back part of what they had committed to give to the apostles to share with their fellow believers and then lied about it. John's disciples were selfishly jealous of Jesus' disciples because Jesus drew larger crowds than John did (John 3:26). It is sad that these followers of Jesus were selfish, but it is good to know that, even though they were selfish, Jesus didn't reject them. Instead, He continued to work with and teach them. God later used many of them in great ways, and He will do the same with us.

God does not give up on us just because we are selfish, have other weaknesses, or have sinned. Peter denied even knowing Jesus three times, yet after he repented, he was forgiven and went on to become a faithful leader in the early church (Matthew 26:69–75). The apostle Paul (previously called Saul), who was not one of the twelve disciples, attended and encouraged the stoning of Stephen (Acts 22:20). But after a powerful encounter with Jesus while on his way to persecute and jail Christians (Acts 9:1–18), began preaching and declaring that Jesus is the Son of God. He was radically changed, and God soon began using him mightily to minister to people in the early church and to write approximately two-thirds of the New Testament.

God chooses and uses the foolish things of this world to confound the wise so that no one can glory in His presence (1 Corinthians 1:27, 29 KJV). If this were not true, He certainly would not have chosen me. No matter how bad we are, if we are willing to change, God will work with us and use us for His glory.

Even in our selfishness, God is gracious to us. Jesus is a High Priest who understands our weaknesses and infirmities because He was "tempted in every way, just as we are—yet he did not sin" (Hebrews 4:15 NIV). Because of this we can go boldly to His throne in prayer and receive the grace we need to meet every need we have (Hebrews 4:16).

Don't ever believe that God can't use you because you have made mistakes. That is a lie that the devil wants you to believe. No matter how many failures you've had, God is always willing to give you a fresh start.

> *Don't believe God can't use you because you've made mistakes.*

The Good Samaritan

Other than the biblical accounts of Jesus giving His life for us, the story of the Good Samaritan (Luke 10:30–37) may be one of the Bible's best examples of unselfishness. While a man was traveling, he was badly beaten and left for dead by robbers. He was lying on the side of the road, desperately in need of help. A priest and a Levite (both religious men) saw the man but crossed to the other side of the road to walk past him. But a Samaritan traveling near the man noticed him and had compassion on him. He poured oil and wine on his wounds and bandaged them. He then put the wounded man on his own donkey, took him to an inn, and took care of him. The next day, the Samaritan had to leave, so he gave the innkeeper some money to let the man stay there, telling him that when he returned he would reimburse the innkeeper for any extra money he had spent on the man.

One of the lessons we can learn from this story is that Jesus does not always ask us to do things when they are convenient for us. The Samaritan was going somewhere. His journey was apparently important enough that he had to continue traveling the next day, yet he did stop to help the injured man. He unselfishly took time to dress the man's wounds and take him to an inn, where he personally took care of him for the night. When he had to leave, he gave the innkeeper his own money, and he promised to repay anything else the innkeeper needed to spend on him. I was impacted by the fact that he didn't put any limits on what he was willing to do.

How often are you and I like the religious men who passed by on the other side of the road when we encounter someone who needs help? We often have a plan and a schedule, and we don't want to be interrupted. But Jesus let people interrupt Him all the time. He always stopped for those who were hurting.

Jesus always stopped for those who were hurting.

In our society today, we see many people standing on street corners begging for money and carrying signs declaring their need. Some are genuine, yet others have found they can make a lot of money panhandling. Sometimes it is difficult to tell the difference between the legitimately needy and those who are simply trying to scam people. I want to help the ones who are genuinely in need, so I pray that God will give me discernment and just try to follow my heart. I don't give to someone who is begging for money while talking on their cell phone with their boom box sitting next to them. I think this example is important because I don't want you to think you are being selfish if you don't help everyone you know or see who has a need. There are times when, if we keep helping someone, we only enable them to continue depending on others instead of doing what they should do for themselves.

I have discovered that if the devil can't get me to do nothing, he will try to get me to do too much. What God wants is for us to have balance, discernment, and wisdom. If you truly have a desire to help people, God will show who you should help.

A Time for Everything

Ecclesiastes 3 teaches us that there is a time for everything, and everything is beautiful in its time (vv. 1, 11). Verse 6 mentions that there is "a time to keep and a time to cast away." Similarly, I believe there's a time to say yes to people's requests and a time to say no. But when God asks us to do something, the only proper answer is always yes. Even if you think you have something more important to do, if you obey God, He will always help you accomplish everything you need to do.

One of our big excuses for not helping others is that we are busy. But are we really too busy to obey God? I doubt it. When we travel, we

> Can you really be too busy to obey God?

can hang a "do not disturb" sign on our hotel room door, but we should never wear an invisible one around our necks. If you want to serve God with all your heart, get ready to be interrupted at times.

The Bible says that people plan their course, but God establishes their steps (Proverbs 16:9 NIV). It is good to have a plan because without one, we usually just waste our time. But our plan should always be secondary to God's plan for us. Tell the Lord that you are willing for Him to interrupt you anytime He wants to and that you will lay aside your plan and follow His.

When God called me to teach His Word, I had three teenagers and a baby. I was making my bed and listening to a recorded teaching one morning when suddenly, without warning, God spoke to me that I would go all over the world and teach His Word. From that time until this, teaching His Word has been my passion, but it wasn't in my plan when God called me. Just imagine starting a ministry with three teenagers and a baby—and, I might add, *no money*.

Obeying God has changed not only my life, but my entire family's lives. Following God can be interesting and quite exciting if you are not addicted to your plan. When Jesus called His disciples, they were all doing something. But when He called, they immediately left their occupations and followed Him.

> Don't offer yourself to God unless you are willing to be inconvenienced.

Don't offer yourself to God for His service unless you are willing to be inconvenienced. You must also be ready to do things you may not understand at the moment. Understanding what God is doing is not nearly as important as obedience. I doubt Hosea understood when God told him to marry a prostitute named Gomer and have children with her (Hosea 1:2), but he did it in obedience to God. In case you are wondering why God would ask someone to do something like this, He used it as a way of showing Israel their great sin and His great love for them. Gomer turned out to be a cheating wife, and God told Hosea to take her back. He wanted people to see this and realize how merciful He is with us by forgiving us and taking us back even though we have sinned.

I doubt Isaiah understood why God wanted him to walk around for years naked and preach (Isaiah 20:3), but this was a sign that the Assyrians would overcome Egypt and Ethiopia. It also symbolized that all the prisoners (regardless of age) would march into captivity completely naked.

Talk about extreme obedience. I think Hosea and Isaiah are great examples of it. I must say that I am glad I live in New Testament times instead of the times when Hosea and Isaiah were alive. The things God has asked me to do seem fairly mild compared to what they were asked to do.

Prefer Others above Yourself

Be devoted to one another in love. Honor one another above yourselves.

Romans 12:10 NIV

The New International Version of the Bible uses the word *honor* in reference to the way we think and act toward other people, and the King James Version says "preferring one another." What does this look like in practicality? Consider these situations:

- If you are in a grocery store checkout line and an elderly person is behind you, let them go ahead of you. Do the same for a mother with two children or for someone with fewer items than you have.
- If you and another person are waiting for the same parking place, let the other person have it (ouch). Parking places are difficult to give up.

- Listen to the person you are with instead of doing all of the talking in a conversation.
- I would say, "Let your spouse have the remote control to the television," but I'm not there yet, so I'd better not give advice I'm not taking (☺).
- When you are the leader of a project and other people are working with you, and you get compliments about the work, make sure you show honor to the people who helped you. Always give credit where credit is due.
- Let people who are waiting to get into a line of traffic merge in ahead of you.

There are many ways we can prefer others, but selfishness will prevent us from doing so unless we are determined to live unselfishly. One night, Dave and I were driving to a church where I had a speaking engagement and were running late because we got stopped by a long train. Dave stopped to let a couple of cars into the line of traffic ahead of us, and I said, "Dave, we don't have time to do that!" He said, "I'm just trying to be nice," to which I replied, "I don't have time to be nice! I have to get to church!" Dave got a good, hard laugh, and I got to embarrassingly tell on myself during the church service. But this is a good example of how we think and act sometimes.

Many things Jesus tells us to do are thwarted by selfishness, so again, I say we must be determined to break the power of selfishness in our lives. You or I might be in a grocery store line, and in our spirit, we hear a whisper to let the person behind us go ahead of us, but our flesh will speak up

> The flesh never runs out of excuses.

also and say "Why should I do that?" or "I would, but I'm in a hurry." The flesh never runs out of excuses to avoid doing what

God wants us to do. But He doesn't want our excuses; He wants our obedience.

Second Timothy 3:1–5 (ESV) paints a stark picture of what the church will be like in the last days before Christ returns:

> But understand this, that in the last days there will come times of difficulty. For people will be lovers of self, lovers of money, proud, arrogant, abusive, disobedient to their parents, ungrateful, unholy, heartless, unappeasable, slanderous, without self-control, brutal, not loving good, treacherous, reckless, swollen with conceit, lovers of pleasure rather than lovers of God, having the appearance of godliness, but denying its power. Avoid such people.

This description of people in the last days is quite discouraging. They are characterized as:

- lovers of self
- lovers of money
- proud
- arrogant
- abusive
- disobedient to their parents
- ungrateful
- unholy
- heartless
- unappeasable
- slanderous
- without self-control
- brutal
- not loving good

- treacherous
- reckless
- swollen with conceit
- lovers of pleasure rather than lovers of God
- having the appearance of godliness but denying its power

We can easily read 2 Timothy 3:1–5 without actually taking time to really think about each specific description of what people will be like in the last days. Many things on this list, if not all of them, we see in our world today. If this Scripture passage describes how the church will be, just imagine how bad the world will be. People who do not know the truth of God's Word will accept this as normal behavior, and each generation that learns to behave this way will only get worse. I don't see any answer other than for Christians to get serious and declare war on selfishness because most of the things on this list are provoked by selfishness and pride. The passage ends with the admonition to avoid such people. We can avoid other people, but we cannot avoid ourselves, so if we are the ones behaving this way, we have a problem.

We should be a light to the world and an example of godly behavior, yet not become entangled with them and learn their ways. We want to teach by our examples and not merely our words.

I truly believe that if every Christian—not just a few, but every Christian—would go into their little piece of the world and let the Holy Spirit help them develop and display the opposite of what this list depicts, we could change the world. People could be selfless, enjoy their money while also using it to further the spread of the gospel and help hurting people, be humble, obey authority, show gratitude, live holy lives, love others, forgive, believe the best of everyone, exercise self-control, be kind, love good, be gentle, be careful and prudent, love God more than anything, and display the power of the gospel.

It is time for us to get serious about how we live and how we represent Jesus in society. It is time to declare war not only on selfishness but also on all other fruits of the flesh. It is time to learn how to be led by the Holy Spirit moment by moment in our daily lives. We are living in serious and desperate times, and getting serious about being a Jesus kind of Christian is not something we can afford to put off.

Being a Christian involves much more than going to church. It means being a follower of Jesus Christ, following in His footsteps, and learning to behave as He did.

CHAPTER 14

Be Determined and Relentless

*Let us not grow weary or become discouraged in doing good,
for at the proper time we will reap, if we do not give in.*

Galatians 6:9 AMP

I found some interesting but sad information when I searched for articles about selfishness. I discovered many articles that said selfishness is good, moral, and a virtue. These indicated that if you don't make yourself number one, you will never succeed in life.

Of course, if we know God's Word, we know that the world's values are different from the values of God's kingdom. But millions of people don't know the truth of God's Word, and even many Christians don't know much about it. The Bible is our handbook on how to live if we want to please God, be happy, enjoy peace, have good relationships, and prosper in all we do. The principles in God's Word work. I, and millions of others, have tried them. We have put them to the test and know we can depend on them. For years, I tried the world's way and was miserable and desperate and had no hope of change. But thankfully, God revealed His Word to me and gave me the grace to actually put it to work in my life, and I am forever changed. One of the most important lessons I have learned in God's Word is that to be selfish is to be miserable. The main theme of the Bible is to love God with all your heart, soul, mind, and strength and to love your neighbor as you love yourself (Matthew 22:37–40). But this is impossible to do if we are filled with selfishness and do nothing to combat it or refuse to give it the right to dominate our lives.

> *To be selfish is to be miserable.*

Defeating selfishness requires change, and sadly, not all Christians are interested in changing. I recently read part of an article about a pastor who quit the ministry after ten years. He said the main reason he quit was that, in his experience, he saw that most

Christians don't want to grow. They want to go to church and simply be told they are doing well where they are. He said they want to be comforted, encouraged, and told they are loved, but they don't want to be told they need to grow spiritually. There are, of course, Christians who are serious about their relationship with God and want to mature spiritually, but in this pastor's experience, they are few compared to those who are content to stay where they are. This is so sad, and I believe it is part of the reason the church is not having the impact it should have in the world.

Defeating selfishness takes determination because, like pride, it is a powerful and relentless force. Unless we are also relentless, we won't win the battle against self-centered selfishness. We will live according to what we want, what we think, and how we feel. If what we want, think, and feel don't agree with God's Word, it will lead us to destruction. The world may promise that we will be happy if we get our way in everything, but actually, the opposite is true.

> *Like pride, selfishness is a powerful and relentless force.*

Why is it so important for us not to be selfish? It is important because, as I mentioned, the central message of God's Word is that we should love Him and love others as we love ourselves, and that is impossible to do if we are selfish. Selfishness blocks and hinders love. When I talk about love, I'm not talking about the romantic love we might feel for a special person or the love we feel for family and friends; I am talking about the unconditional love God shows us. God's kind of love requires sacrifice and must be made available to everyone, even our enemies.

> *God's kind of love requires sacrifice.*

Many people just go to church each week and think that's all they need to do to walk with God. But we go to church to learn what to do, and then we should go out and do it.

Are You Determined?

To be determined means to make a firm, quality decision and be resolved to follow through. Think about it this way: It's easy to go on a diet on Sunday evening right after dinner, but what happens about noon the next day when hunger sets in? People who are determined don't change their mind about their decisions. They press through difficulties and go all the way through to the finish line.

In Psalm 51:10 David prays that God will "renew a right, persevering, and steadfast spirit" in him. *Endurance, perseverance, effort, determination, relentlessness, steadfastness*—these are words we rarely hear sermons about or choose to read about, but without these character qualities we will have a mediocre life at best and possibly a life marked by failure.

I want to be clear that we cannot do anything God asks us to do by willpower alone. We need to exercise our will and our free choice, but we need the strength and guidance of the Holy Spirit to accomplish anything meaningful. People who don't depend on God and His amazing grace may accomplish things, but they will not have peace and real joy in those achievements. Likewise, people who depend solely on God to do everything and don't take action themselves don't accomplish anything, either. God works through us, but He won't do everything for us.

God works through you, but He won't do everything for you.

Paul was determined to know Jesus and have an intimate relationship with Him. You can sense his passionate desire in Philippians 3:10–11:

[For my determined purpose is] that I may know Him [that I may progressively become more deeply and intimately acquainted with Him, perceiving and recognizing and understanding the wonders of His Person more strongly and more clearly], and that I may in that same way come to know the power outflowing from His resurrection [which it exerts over believers], and that I may so share His *sufferings* as to be continually transformed [in spirit into His likeness even] to His death, [in the hope] that if possible I may attain to the [spiritual and moral] resurrection [that lifts me] out from among the dead [even while in the body]. (emphasis mine)

Paul understood that he would experience some suffering in order to obtain the transformation and intimate relationship with God he desired. When was the last time you heard a sermon on being willing

You may experience suffering to enjoy the intimate relationship with God you desire.

to suffer in order to do God's will? Suffering isn't a popular sermon topic, but if people are to mature spiritually and be all God wants them to be, it is necessary. I am not referring to suffering disease, tragedy, or other desperately painful circumstances, but to the suffering we endure in our flesh when we deny it the right to control us, and choose to obey God instead.

For example, if my husband and I are having a heated discussion about something we don't agree on and I can tell it is going to turn into an argument, and the Holy Spirit whispers to me to stop trying to push my opinion and just be quiet, if I obey Him, my flesh will hurt. Our pride doesn't like to let someone else think they are right when we believe they are wrong. We want to convince them to agree with us, and those conversations often turn into arguments.

Paul (formerly Saul) was also determined to let go of the past and press forward to the future (Philippians 3:12–14). I am sure that the devil reminded Paul of his past life and tried to make him feel guilty and condemned, but Paul was determined to not live in the past. We should have this same type of determination. We lose a lot of time feeling guilty about things for which God has forgiven us. I suffered terribly with guilt for many years, and once I learned the truth of God's Word, I had to be determined and relentless in my pursuit of freedom from guilt.

I am determined to finish the race God has set before me. I want to finish all that God has called me to do. At times, this requires pressing through difficult circumstances, but I am determined, and that determination is like fuel that keeps me going.

Success and Victory Demand Determination

> But Daniel determined in his heart that he would not defile himself by [eating his portion of] the king's rich and dainty food or by [drinking] the wine which he drank; therefore he requested of the chief of the eunuchs that he might [be allowed] not to defile himself.
>
> Daniel 1:8

Daniel, a young man mentioned in the Old Testament, was determined not to defile himself by doing what God didn't want him to do. He had made a vow to God to eat only vegetables and drink only water for a period of time. But when he was taken into the king's palace to serve him, his training included eating rich food. He asked the man in charge if he could keep his commitment to God and eat only vegetables and water, telling him that at the end of ten days, he would be healthier than the men eating the royal food. He was given permission because God gave him favor. He did indeed end up healthier on His God-ordained diet than the people on the diet the king offered (Daniel 1:8–16). I share this story to show that Daniel was a man of his word. He was determined to keep his vow to God. He also had an excellent spirit, and he was promoted over many others because of these virtues (Daniel 5:12; 6:1–3 NKJV).

Another person of determination in the Bible is King Solomon. He wanted to build a temple for God, and 2 Chronicles 2:1 says, "Solomon *determined* to build a temple for the Name of the Lord and a royal capitol" (emphasis mine).

In addition, the apostle Paul wrote that he was determined not to know anything else except Jesus and Him crucified (1 Corinthians 2:2 NKJV). Surely, he had a great deal of determination in order to continue going from place to place to preach the Word of God. He endured great hardship, hunger, imprisonment, shipwreck, discouragement, destitution, and many other difficulties (2 Corinthians 11:23–29), but he endeavored to finish his life's course with joy. He writes in Acts 20:24, "But none of these things move me; nor do I count my life dear to myself, so that I may finish my race with joy, and the ministry which I have received from the Lord Jesus, to testify to the gospel of the grace of God" (NKJV).

Paul's difficulties did not entice him to give up, because he had made a quality decision. He was determined. If you want to reach any goal that you have, whether it is a spiritual one or a practical one, you must keep your eyes on the finish line and not allow yourself to get entangled with the problems you encounter on your journey.

To be relentless you must never give up or give in. Be strong and intense, and keep up the pace required to reach the finish line.

You must never give up or give in.

Ask and Receive

Whatever you ask for in prayer, believe (trust and be confident) that it is granted to you, and you will [get it].

Mark 11:24

Mark 11:24 is an encouraging scripture with a promise that is hard to believe. Can we really ask for whatever we want and get it if we believe we will? Anything we ask for must be based on God's Word, but if it is, God promises we will get it. But notice that He doesn't say *when* it will manifest in our lives. This is the hard part. We ask, then we wait, and then we receive, but not until God's perfect time.

The question we all have is "How long will I have to wait?" God doesn't tell us, because it is during the waiting time that our faith is tested. Trust always requires waiting on God. It requires patience. I am sure most of us are waiting on something right now. I know I am, and it is up to us to decide whether we enjoy the wait through being patient and resting in God or make ourselves miserable through impatience and frustration.

If you study the word for *patience* in the original Greek language in which the Bible was originally written, you will find that patience can only grow under trial.[15] Patience is not merely the ability to wait, but the attitude with which we wait. All of us will wait. Waiting is part of life, and there is no getting away from it. We wait in the doctor's office, we wait at the dentist's office, we wait in traffic, and we wait for God to answer our prayers. But what kind of attitude do we wait with? Do we wait with patience? Or do we wait with frustration, anger, negativity, or an attitude of giving up?

Consider these two verses about patience:

> For you have need of steadfast patience and endurance,
> so that you may perform and fully accomplish the will
> of God, and thus receive and carry away [and enjoy to
> the full] what is promised.
>
> Hebrews 10:36

> But let endurance and steadfastness and patience have
> full play and do a thorough work, so that you may be
> [people] perfectly and fully developed [with no defects],
> lacking in nothing.
>
> James 1:4

Sometimes circumstances seem so impossible that people think you are crazy to keep going. Success doesn't come overnight. It takes a long time and a lot of hard work. It may take failing many times and trying again and again. The writer of Ecclesiastes said a dream comes to pass with "much business and painful effort" (Ecclesiastes 5:3).

> The greatest oak was once a little nut who held its ground.
> —Author unknown

I can't even count the number of times I felt like a nut for believing I could reach my goals in ministry, but by God's grace, I kept pushing forward, many times so slowly I felt I was not moving at all. But God is faithful, and now I am here and still determined to finish my course with joy, as Paul was committed to doing (Acts 20:24). Some people dream of success, but others wake up and work hard at it. I think determination is continuing to put one foot in front of the other, even when you feel sure you may fail. As newspaper columnist Ann Landers said, "Nobody ever drowned in his own sweat."[16]

Don't just dream of success; wake up and work for it.

In this book we are not dealing with a dream for our life in general, but a desire to be free from selfishness; however, the same principles work either way. Whatever your dream is, I pray you have enough determination to reach it.

Do You Have a Handicap?

When I use the term *handicap*, I am not talking about a physical handicap but about some type of deficit that makes it difficult for you to reach your goal. For example, my natural temperament is a handicap when it comes to being unselfish or patient. As I have mentioned, I have a strong, aggressive, type A, choleric personality. It serves me well when it comes to getting things done or reaching my goals, but it gets in my way when it comes to being selfless and serving others or being patient, especially with people who don't communicate in the way you would prefer them to communicate. Most type A personalities are determined to get what they want, and that works if what we want is what God wants. But it becomes a handicap when it comes to being unselfish, because I want what I want, and I want other people in my life to help me get it. This sounds bad, but at least I know the truth about myself, and it helps me resist the temptation to be that way when I need to.

We cannot use "That's just the way I am" as an excuse for not changing, because our excuses are just that to God: excuses! Several years ago, I read a book by Tim LaHaye called *The Spirit-Controlled Temperament*, which helped me greatly. In this book, he explains that everyone is born with a temperament. The temperaments fall into four general categories, and you can read about them in many places: the strong choleric, the fun-loving sanguine, the laid-back phlegmatic, and the deep, creative, but often dark melancholy.

Each temperament has its strengths and weaknesses. People usually have one dominant temperament and a little bit of one or more of the others. For example, our youngest son is choleric and sanguine. This means he can get a lot done and is a hard worker, but he also knows how to have a good time. I, on the other hand, am almost totally choleric. Dave is phlegmatic, which means he is easygoing and doesn't worry about things. Our other son is highly choleric, as I am, and one of our daughters is a mix of sanguine and melancholy. The other daughter is phlegmatic and very adaptable. When my children were growing up, we had four of them with different temperaments, and until I found Tim LaHaye's book, it was war in our house most of the time.

LaHaye's purpose in the book is to show that no matter what our natural temperament is, we can use our strengths and learn how to let the Holy Spirit help us control our weaknesses. We can either allow our temperaments to take their natural course, or we can submit them to the Holy Spirit's control. For me, this means that if I want to be unselfish or patient, I will need a lot of help from the Holy Spirit. Over the years, I have become more balanced, and I think that when I am being Spirit-controlled, I am a good mix of all the temperaments. Without the Holy Spirit's help, I will get a job done, but I might hurt a lot of people's feelings in the process. I tend to be so focused on what I am trying to accomplish that I can forget to even use good manners. But if I am being Spirit-controlled, I can get the job done, while walking in love and thinking of others, instead of just thinking of what I am trying to do. It is good to know ourselves!

Know your strengths and your weaknesses, and ask for help with the weaknesses. Love calls us to care about others' interests; to be gentle, kind, humble, and patient; and to express many other good qualities we can't express unless we are Spirit-controlled.

I desperately need the help of the Holy Spirit continually. How about you?

> You need the help of the Holy Spirit.

Zacchaeus

In Luke 19:1–5, we read about Zacchaeus, a man who was small in stature (short, physically), who heard that Jesus was entering

Jericho, and he wanted to see Him. By profession, Zacchaeus was
a tax collector, meaning that he worked for the Roman govern-
ment. Many tax collectors were hated because after they collected
the government's required monies, they often added more to keep
for themselves.

The crowd was large, and Zacchaeus knew he would not be able
to see Jesus over them, so instead of just giving up and saying,
"I'm so short there's no point in even trying to see Jesus," he ran
ahead and climbed a sycamore tree. When Jesus reached the spot
where Zacchaeus was, He looked up. What caused Him to look up
at that precise time and place? Perhaps Jesus admired Zacchaeus's
determination. Jesus told him to come down immediately and
then said, "I must stay at your house today" (v. 5).

Wow! Jesus wanted to go to a tax collector's house. Of all the
religious people in the crowd, He chose a hated tax collector to
visit at home.

Since he was willing to climb a tree just to see Jesus, Zacchaeus
must have wanted to change. He exerted extra effort to get what
he wanted, and Jesus respects people who do that. Maybe climb-
ing a tree was easy for Zacchaeus, but I think it would be dif-
ficult for me. If you need to, are you willing to climb a tree or do
whatever it takes to be all God wants you to be? Jesus' visit to
Zacchaeus was a life-changing event for him. He suddenly wanted
to repay everything he had stolen four times over and give half
of what he had to the poor (Luke 19:8). One visit from God can
change us forever.

Be Relentless

Mark 10:46–52 tells us the story of a blind man named Barti-
maeus who was relentless in asking Jesus to heal him. As Jesus

and a large crowd with Him were leaving Jericho, Bartimaeus sat by the roadside begging. When he heard that Jesus was passing by, he cried out, "Jesus, Son of David, have mercy on me!" (v. 47 NIV). Many people rebuked Bartimaeus and told him to be quiet, but he shouted all the more, "Son of David, have mercy on me!" (v. 48 NIV). Bartimaeus's relentless cries for mercy got Jesus' attention! Jesus stopped and asked the blind man what he wanted Him to do for him. Bartimaeus replied, "Rabbi, I want to see" (v. 51 NIV), and Jesus fully restored his sight.

Bartimaeus was determined to be able to ask Jesus to heal him. Everyone told him to keep quiet, but he just kept loudly calling for Jesus to have mercy on him. Have you ever gotten excited about Jesus and had the religious people around you tell you to calm down and be quiet? I have. The devil hates it when people are enthusiastic about Jesus. When I first got excited about Jesus, people told me I was just being emotional. Even if I was, what's wrong with expressing our excitement about Jesus with our emotions? People get emotionally excited at football games, and nobody thinks anything is wrong with that, so why can't we get excited about Jesus?

I am glad that when Bartimaeus was told to be quiet, he shouted even louder than before. Maybe to the people standing around Bartimaeus, he seemed a little ridiculous, but he got his miracle.

Like many other people God is using for His purposes today, I am not qualified in the natural sense of the word. I don't have enough education. I think education is great, and I encourage you to pursue it if you can, but it does not necessarily qualify a person to be used by God. I almost failed English class, and now my television program is aired in two-thirds of the world in more than 110 languages, as of the writing of this book. By the time you read it, that number will have grown. I didn't go to seminary. No one has ever taught me how to put a sermon together. I have never taken a public speaking class, but God has qualified me by His choice and anointing, and He has given me a relentless determination to pursue what He has called me to do, and that is all any one of us needs.

CHAPTER 15

Discover the Power of Caring for Others

Let each of you esteem and look upon and be concerned for not [merely] his own interests, but also each for the interests of others.

Philippians 2:4

If you have made it this far in the book, I can safely assume that you are ready to move beyond frequently asking "What about me?" I trust you are ready to serve God with all your heart, even if it means sacrificing what you want in order to care for others.

Selfish people are only concerned for their own interests; they are even willing to hurt other people in order to get what they want. But we can see from Philippians 2:4 that God wants us to be concerned not just for ourselves, but also for the interests of others.

When Jesus' disciples were arguing about which of them was the greatest, Jesus said that the greatest of all is the servant of all (Luke 22:24–27). He said He didn't come to earth to be served but to serve (Matthew 20:28).

In John 13:1–17, we see a beautiful account of Jesus, the Son of God, taking off His garment, putting on a servant's towel, and bending down to wash His disciples' feet. Knowing where He came from and where He was going, He put on the servant's towel and began to wash their feet. He could wash their feet because He knew who He was. People who are insecure and really don't know who they are in Christ have a difficult time serving, because they feel the need to impress others. Serving doesn't always impress people, but it does impress God. I don't think any of us is truly free until we no longer feel the need to impress anyone.

> You will never be truly free until you no longer feel the need to impress anyone.

I find it interesting that, when Jesus went to wash Peter's feet, Peter resisted and said he should be the one washing Jesus' feet. Jesus replied, "If I do not wash you, you have no part with Me" (John 13:8 NKJV). This is a powerful statement that reveals why many relationships fail. If we don't serve one another, then we have no part in one another. Relationships that are one-sided almost always fail. If one person does all the giving while the other does all the taking, they have an unhealthy and unsustainable relationship.

Let me encourage you to pause for a moment and ask yourself what you do for the people you are in relationship with. Because of the selfishness in our human nature, it is easier to be takers rather than the givers God wants us to be.

In John 13:17, Jesus says, "If you know these things, blessed and happy and to be envied are you if you practice them [if you act accordingly and really do them]." We must be careful not to become proud of ourselves simply because we know things. Knowledge is wonderful, but putting knowledge into action is what's really important. There is no power in knowing without action to back it up.

In a marriage or a friendship, each partner should do things for the other. Dave and I have been married since 1967, and we still make an effort to do things for one another because we know that this is one way to keep a marriage strong. I have had one-sided relationships with people who called themselves friends. But people who do all of the taking and none of the giving are not really friends, and I don't want any more relationships like that.

I am the president of Joyce Meyer Ministries, but this doesn't mean I am too important to serve others. Servant leaders are the best leaders of all, and they provide a great example to those who are younger and will eventually become leaders. It is useless to tell others what to do and then not do it ourselves. I frequently take a survey of my life and consider what I am doing for other people beyond my job in ministry. I want to live my private life the way I tell people to live theirs in my teachings. We should pray for and look for opportunities to help and serve others.

I have a job to do, and God has given me people who help me in order for that to happen. I cannot spend all of my time serving because I have to preach, study, write, travel, and do television. And actually, all of these involve serving those who need to hear God's Word. But, when I have opportunity, it is good for me to serve in small but important practical ways, because it reminds me that I am no more important than anyone else. We should never ask someone else to do something that we wouldn't do ourselves if we could.

Power in Serving

The Greek word for *servant* conveys the idea of subjection without bondage.[17] If I am your servant, I can submit to you without feeling I am in bondage or that I have lost my freedom.

I think many people view being a servant as being in a lowly position, but God sees it as the opposite. True servants must be confident and secure. They must know who they are in Christ. They are not looking for a title or a position that others regard as important. They simply love God and want to help people.

God gifts some people as helpers, and for these people, serving is not hard. They often have to resist saying yes to everyone who needs help so they can maintain balance in their lives. Those of us who are not gifted in this area will have to help others intentionally.

There is power in serving. Those who humble themselves will be exalted (1 Peter 5:6). The humbling is challenging, but the exalting is lots of fun. Just remember, we don't get the exalting without first humbling ourselves under God's mighty hand. If you are not accustomed to living a servant lifestyle, it might be hard to believe that if you give up what you want in order to serve someone else it will increase your joy, but I know from my own experience that it does.

Consider how learning to serve others changed Darrell's life:

I woke up at five a.m. sharp. Like most days, I was due in court in a few hours to plead my client's case. Bleary-eyed, I started my coffee and began flipping through TV channels to see what was happening in the world.

The law was my life—my passion. But I felt adrift, listless, and even depressed, as though something was missing. I believed in God and once enjoyed a close relationship with Him, but somewhere along the way I let Him slip out of my life.

Remote in hand, I changed the channel and was met with a woman preaching God's Word to a crowded auditorium. God used that program to pull me out of the hole and change my life. It's a miracle.

I began regularly studying Scripture and learning principles from God's Word. God filled the void in my life and gave me a renewed joy, passion, and purpose.

Today, I serve as a legal arbitrator, and I credit my success to time in God's Word. My family says I'm a better listener, and I'm definitely more generous. In fact, the more I give to others, the more I have! It has changed who I am. I have become a thankful giver.

Before, I was a little too "What about me? What about me? What's in it for me?" But God brought me back. I've learned that you can't be happy and selfish at the same time—you have to do something for someone else."

I Die Daily

In 1 Corinthians 15:31 Paul writes, "I die daily." He meant that he faced the possibility of physical death each day because of his commitment to preach the gospel, but I also believe he meant that every day he had to say no to himself and yes to God.

Dying to self means that we do things we would rather not do, and we learn to do them with a good attitude. It does no good to serve others and then have the attitude of a martyr or feel we are being taken advantage of. Neither does it do any good to serve others and then sit and think we are good because we did it.

Sometimes, even when we know it is right to die daily and serve others, we forget to do it because we get so busy. God's Word encourages us not to do this: "And do not forget to do good and to share with others, for with such sacrifices God is pleased" (Hebrews 13:16 NIV). I ask God daily to show me what I can do for others. He doesn't always show me something, but at least He knows I am willing. I believe doing things for other people on purpose is what helps us fight selfishness and keeps us from becoming like the world.

Watch for Needs and Meet Them

Develop the habit of paying attention to what people say they want and need. Recently I mentioned in a group of people that I had been looking for a very specific type of black purse. I wanted outside pockets and inside pockets, and I wanted it to zip. About two hours later, one of the women in the group showed up with the exact purse I had been looking for as a gift for me. She had listened to me and went searching for what I wanted. Receiving the gift brought me joy, and I could tell that giving it brought her joy too. It was interesting that I had looked for the purse for more than a year, and she found it in two hours. I think God sometimes hides things

> Pay attention to what people say they want and need.

from some people but shows them to others simply because He wants them to bless someone else.

I love Acts 10:38, which says, "God anointed Jesus of Nazareth with the Holy Spirit and with power, who went about doing good and healing all who were oppressed by the devil" (NKJV). Jesus used His power to be a blessing to others, and my personal opinion is that this increased His power. Not only do we increase our power through doing things for others, but God gives back to us what we give to others multiplied many times over. Anne Frank said, "No one has ever become poor from giving."[18]

A Random Act of Kindness

Unexpected joy came to me through an opportunity to be a blessing to a total stranger. Dave and I had gone to eat in a restaurant where the service was extremely slow. When the server finally arrived at our table, she apologized for the delay and explained they were short-staffed. As we talked with her, she shared that she was working double shifts six days a week because she had gotten behind on her bills while the restaurant had been closed for a period of time during the COVID-19 pandemic. She said she had a young daughter and was concerned that her power would be disconnected if she couldn't pay her bill. We gave her a generous tip, but after we left the restaurant, the Lord began dealing with me about paying her electric bill.

I planned to send my daughter to the restaurant to make arrangements to pay the bill, but I felt God wanted me to do it myself. The next day, I went back to the restaurant, but the server was off that day. The hostess recognized me and told me how much I had helped her, so I asked if she would like to help me with something. She said yes, so I told her about the server, and she knew immediately who I was talking about. I gave her my daughter's email address and asked her to give it to the waitress and tell her that if she would send the electric bill to us, we would pay the entire bill. She did send it with a zealous thank-you, and we paid the bill, which was several hundred dollars. We have never seen the server again, but I still remember the joy I received from being able to take a burden off of her, and all it took was a little time and money.

There are many things we can do for people, even if we don't know them, if we will just listen and be willing to act if God prompts us. Live to give, not to get, and you will be a happy person. You can hear the stories about the joy other people find in giving, but the only way you will prove it is to do it yourself. You might say, "I don't have enough money to be able to pay someone's electric bill." God doesn't expect you to do something you can't do. But instead of thinking about what you can't do, think of what you can do. Even if you can give somebody a small portion of what they need, you will please God and receive the reward of happiness.

Being a servant releases God's power. In Acts 6:1–8 the twelve apostles turned the daily task of serving and waiting on tables over to Stephen and some others who were qualified. The Bible states that great miracles took place through Stephen, a person who served others.

> Serving with a good attitude requires great spiritual strength.

Being a servant is a power position. Serving is not a sign of weakness; it requires great spiritual strength to serve with a good attitude.

Another way to minister to others is to lighten their burdens. Galatians 6:2 says that we are to bear one another's burdens. That means we can pray for people, and we can express understanding when they face difficult situations. Sometimes understanding is the best gift we can give someone. We can encourage with words or by meeting a practical need. At other times, one of the best ways we can help someone who is hurting is simply to be there. We don't even always have to say anything, because just being present lets them know we care. I would like to challenge you to see how many unique ways you can serve or give. Be creative and have fun being a blessing to others.

Paul writes in Galatians 6:10: "Therefore, as we have opportunity, let us do good to all people, especially to those who belong to the family of believers" (NIV). The Amplified Bible, Classic Edition refers to this as being "mindful to be a blessing." I urge you to fill your mind with ways you can be a blessing to others. I find that simply the act of thinking about blessing others gives me joy. We should live for that, not for ourselves.

A Simple Way Everyone Can Serve

How many things do you have in your home that you are not using at all and perhaps haven't used for a long, long time? Clothes? Jewelry? Household items? We tend to keep things in case we ever need them, but if you haven't used something in a long time, maybe it would be better to pass it on to someone who could benefit from it. If you have blankets or coats you are not using, there are people living on the streets who would love to have them to keep them warm. If you don't have anyone to give the items to, take them to a shelter or donate them to a responsible charity.

I purposefully go through my closet about once a month and take out items I can give away. My daughter helped me do this a few days ago, and we cleaned out a closet in a bedroom that is seldom used. We found blankets, several pillows, a comforter, and other items we had forgotten we even had. They got boxed up and went to Goodwill. Our flesh loves to own things, but God loves to see us give and give generously.

Serving Is the Fruit of Loving God

In John 21, Jesus asked Peter three times if he loved Him. Each time, Peter said he did, and Jesus replied, "Feed My lambs," "Shepherd (tend) My sheep," and "Feed My sheep" (vv. 15, 16, 17). I believe what He was really saying was "If you love Me, help someone."

The small things we do for people may be big things to God. After Jesus' resurrection, He appeared to His disciples and served them breakfast (John 21:12). Think about it: *The resurrected Lord served breakfast to His disciples.* I find this amazing and encouraging. He apparently thought serving was important.

Jesus did many small things. He "stood still" when he heard two blind men cry for help (Matthew 20:30–32 NKJV). He took time to talk to children (Matthew 19:13–15), and He stopped for hurting people. Jesus stopped for blind Bartimaeus when he cried out for mercy (Mark 10:46–52). He stopped for the woman with the issue of blood (Mark 5:25–34). And He stopped to raise a widow's son from the dead (Luke 7:11–17). Jesus was frequently going somewhere, just as we are. I am sure He was busy, but never too busy to stop for people who were hurting. We are encouraged to study the *steps* of Jesus, but today I encourage you to study the *stops* of Jesus. Don't let your plan be so important that you won't stop to help someone in need.

The only way to conquer selfishness and keep it conquered is to actively be involved in helping others. We spend a lot of time trying to make ourselves happy, but we actually have no ability to make ourselves happy, at least not for very long. Living the most selfish and self-centered life in the world won't make us happy for long. But each time we sow a seed of happiness into someone else's life, God will bring a harvest of happiness into our life. God created us to reach out to others, not to reach inward, trying to get everything we want.

Do Everything for the Lord

Whatever may be your task, work at it heartily (from the soul), as [something done] for the Lord and not for men, knowing [with all certainty] that it is from the Lord [and not from men] that you will receive the inheritance which is your [real] reward. [The One Whom] you are actually serving [is] the Lord Christ (the Messiah).

Colossians 3:23–24

Whether we do something big or something small, we should do it for Jesus and not to impress people, because it is from Him that we will receive our reward.

Everything we do can become a spiritual act if we do it unto the Lord. We think prayer, Bible study, and church attendance are spiritual activities, and they are, but going to the grocery store, doing laundry, and going to work as an office clerk can also be spiritual if, in your heart, you do them for the Lord. Some endeavors may produce more spiritual fruit than others, but everything we do can be spiritual and even holy if done for God.

When I get dressed in the morning, I think about whether I am dressed in a way that will honor God. I want to look good for God, not to impress people. I want to represent Him well. No matter what you do or how ordinary it may seem, try purposefully thinking *I am doing this for You, Lord.*

A simple way to serve God and others is through encouragement. People on every level need to be encouraged: the rich and the poor, those in authority and those under authority, married

people and single people, those with children and those who have
no children. I cannot think of even one category of people who
don't need encouragement. Encouragement gives people courage
to press on. Life is hard on everyone, and you never know when
a simple word of encouragement or a compliment may change
someone's day. Many people are hurting, but they don't act as
though they are. We have gotten good at pretending everything
is okay when it isn't. People are often afraid to be honest about
how they really feel, because they fear being rejected or judged
critically.

Aim to give the gift of confidence to someone every day. Use
your words to be a blessing to people. Words are extremely pow-
erful (Proverbs 18:21). Make someone else happy, and it will make
you happy too.

Another simple way to serve others is to genuinely listen to
them. Many times people just need someone to talk to. Some peo-
ple talk too much, and we cannot let them monopolize all our
time, but if we are sensitive to the Holy Spirit, we will know when
we need to take time to just listen.

One time I was waiting in a doctor's office and an elderly man
was sitting near me. I had taken my Bible and planned to read and
pray in the waiting room, and this man was preventing me from
being spiritual like I wanted to be. I felt a bit irritated with him
when suddenly God whispered in my heart, "If this man were
Billy Graham, would you listen to him?"

I knew immediately what God was saying to me. I didn't want
to listen to the man in the doctor's office because there was noth-
ing in it for me, but had he been Billy Graham or some other per-
son I deemed "important," I would have listened and then told
everyone about the important person I spoke with that day. The
elderly man wasn't important to me, but he was important to God,

as is every single person on earth. If we want to work with and for God, this is one of the first lessons we need to learn. I'm happy to say that if that same situation occurred today I would listen to the man, but at the time I was too selfish to do so. I am very grateful for the miracle of change that God works in our lives.

CHAPTER 16

Fight Greed with Generosity

Guard yourselves and keep free from all covetousness (the immoderate desire for wealth, the greedy longing to have more); for a man's life does not consist in and is not derived from possessing overflowing abundance or that which is over and above his needs.

Luke 12:15

Proverbs 1:19 says that greed takes away the life of its possessor. Thank God that when we are born again and His Spirit comes to live in us, we have generosity inside of us. Our new nature wants to be generous, and being generous is the only way I know to fight greed and selfishness.

In Luke 12:16–21, Jesus tells the story of a rich man whose fields yielded such an abundant harvest that he had no place to put it because his barns were already full. He thought about what to do and decided to tear down his barns and build bigger ones for himself. He said, I will have plenty of grain laid up for many years, and I'll eat, drink, and be merry.

Notice that we don't read anything about a desire to use his abundance to be a blessing to other people. I wonder how many of his neighbors had needs he could have met and still had more than enough for himself.

What happened next? God said to him, "You fool! This very night they [the messengers of God] will demand your soul of you; and all the things that you have prepared, whose will they be?" (v. 20). This is a sobering thought and one we should meditate on, because none of us knows how much time we have left on earth. The rich man made decisions thinking he would be around a long, long time, but God told him he wouldn't survive the night. I have to wonder if he would have lived longer had he been a generous man, using his resources to help others.

Multitudes of people spend their lives selfishly saving every penny they can get their hands on and then die before they get a chance to enjoy it. I firmly believe in saving money for your future. It is wise to do so. Proverbs 13:22 says, "A good person leaves an inheritance for their children's children" (NIV). But in addition to preparing for the future, you should also be generous to others and enjoy yourself and the life God has blessed you with. Dave has a simple formula for handling money. He says, "Give some, save some, and spend some within your borders—and God will expand your borders." This formula is balanced, and we need balance in our lives. Excess in any area of life is the devil's playground.

> *Excess in any area of life is the devil's playground.*

Generous People Get God's Attention

The New Testament includes several remarkable stories about people who were generous. I'd like to highlight two of them.

Tabitha

In Acts 9:36–41, we're told of a follower of Jesus named Tabitha (Dorcas in Greek), who was known in her town as a woman who worked hard doing good deeds and helping the poor. But she became sick and died. When the apostle Peter heard about this, he went to her home, knelt beside her, prayed, and then said, "Tabitha, get up!" (v. 40). And she did.

Cornelius

Acts 10 tells the story of a God-fearing Roman centurion named Cornelius who prayed and gave generously to those in need. One day an angel appeared to him and said, "Your prayers and gifts to the poor have come up as a memorial offering before God" (v. 4 NIV). A memorial is something that stands before God as a constant reminder of what someone has done. We have memorials here on earth that are designed for similar purposes.

The angel told Cornelius to send for Simon Peter, also known as the apostle Peter (v. 5). When Cornelius's men asked for Simon

Peter at the house where he was staying, the Holy Spirit said to him, "Three men are looking for you. So get up and go downstairs. Do not hesitate to go with them, for I have sent them" (vv. 19–20 NIV).

Ordinarily, Simon Peter would not have gone to the home of a Gentile, but when he arrived, Cornelius and a large group of people were present (v. 27). While Simon Peter was speaking to the people about God, the Holy Spirit fell on all of them and he baptized them (vv. 44–48).

Christians consider Cornelius the first Gentile convert to Christianity, and Scripture plainly says the angel came because of his prayers and gifts to the poor (v. 4). They stood as a memorial before God, and He remembered Cornelius. You and I can learn from this story that God also remembers our gifts to the poor, and we will be rewarded.

We often talk about the power of God that was present in the early Church. They regularly saw miracles, signs, and wonders. And I believe there is a direct correlation between generosity and God's power. I encourage you to read Acts 4:32–35. This passage teaches us that the early believers were of one heart and mind and shared everything they had (NIV). It teaches us that they were not selfish, and that whenever someone had a need, the generosity of their fellow believers was able to meet it.

God Is Generous

God is generous, and if we want to imitate Him, we need to be generous also. One of the Lord's many names in the Old Testament is *Jehovah-Jireh*, which means "The Lord Will Provide." In Ephesians 3:20, we are encouraged to pray big, bold prayers, because God "is able to do exceedingly abundantly above all that we ask or think" (NKJV).

Our God is not the God of "barely get by," but a generous God who delights in seeing His children blessed in every way. Third John 2 says, "Beloved, I pray that you may prosper in all things and be in health, just as your soul prospers" (NKJV).

God wants our soul to prosper first, meaning that He desires our spiritual maturity, and then He will add other types of prosperity. Spiritual things should always come before material things.

> God wants your soul to prosper first.

God's Word says that if we will bring all the tithes into His storehouse, He will rebuke the devourer for our sake and open the windows of heaven and *pour out* blessings so great we cannot contain them (Malachi 3:10–11, emphasis mine). God doesn't dribble out blessings; He *pours* them out.

According to the Christianpost.com, only 13 percent of evangelical Christians tithe, which means to give a tenth part of something. Based on this statistic, if we believe God's Word, then 87 percent of Christians are missing out on God's blessings.

Some people say that tithing is under the law (limited to Old Testament teaching) and not part of New Testament teaching. Jesus says in Matthew 23:23 and Luke 11:42 that tithing should not be neglected, but He said this before the New Covenant was ratified. For the sake of making a point, let's say that tithing is not required under the New Covenant. Paul instructs Christians to be generous with what they have (2 Corinthians 9:6–11). I like to ask, if the believers under the Old Covenant could give 10 percent under the law, what should you and I be doing by grace? I would think we would certainly give more than the people of Old Testament days did. If we were to be truly generous, I doubt we would ever give less than 10 percent. We would probably give more. I am not trying to convince you to tithe or not to tithe. I mention this merely to make the point that we should always do the *most* we can, not the *least*. We will reap only on what we sow. Dave and I believe in tithing. We do it because we want to, not because we feel we have to. The tithe is a starting point for us, and we love to do many other things in addition to our tithe as needs arise or when we simply want to bless someone.

If you are a parent, you know that you delight in seeing your children blessed and healthy, and you enjoy helping improve their lives and take pressure off of them. If we as parents desire this for our children, how much more does our Father in heaven desire this for us, His children?

> If you, then, though you are evil, know how to give good gifts to your children, how much more will your Father in heaven give good gifts to those who ask him!
>
> Matthew 7:11 NIV

Sowing and Reaping

All farmers know that to reap a harvest, they must sow a seed. God uses this same principle in most areas of our life. Consider these scriptures:

> A man who has friends must himself be friendly, but there is a friend who sticks closer than a brother.
>
> Proverbs 18:24 NKJV

> Blessed are the merciful, for they will be shown mercy.
>
> Matthew 5:7 NIV

> Do not be deceived, God is not mocked; for whatever a man sows, that he will also reap. For he who sows to his

flesh will of the flesh reap corruption, but he who sows
to the Spirit will of the Spirit reap everlasting life. And
let us not grow weary while doing good, for in due sea-
son we shall reap if we do not lose heart.

                                        Galatians 6:7–9 NKJV

These scriptures and others like them show us the kingdom
principle of sowing and reaping, which
God placed in motion from the creation of
the world. If we obey this principle, we will
reap its rewards. God is gracious in giving
us a way to have our desires met, which
is to give away some of what we want. We
should always help the poor, because doing so is close to the heart
of God. When we give to the poor, we lend to the Lord, and the
Lord will pay us back (Proverbs 19:17). Think about what the
Bible says about true religion:

> *Have your desires met by giving away some of what you want.*

Pure and unblemished religion [as it is expressed in
outward acts] in the sight of our God and Father is this:
to visit and look after the fatherless and the widows in
their distress, and to keep oneself uncontaminated by
the [secular] world.

                                        James 1:27 AMP

God seems to have a special place in His heart for the father-
less and the widows. People in both groups would tend to feel lonely
and may have no one to help them. God asks us to help them. Dave
and I know a widow who owns her home but cannot afford to pay
the taxes on it, so several of us get together each year and pay her
taxes. Sometimes we give her gift certificates for groceries or clothing.

Some suggestions of ways to help the fatherless and the widows are to include them in activities that your family is doing, take them to lunch, or buy them a gift they couldn't afford to get themselves. Orphans, widows, and others in need may feel invisible if no one pays attention to them. Simone Weil said, "Attention is the rarest and purest form of generosity."[19]

Helping the poor is super simple. If you know people in need, start with them. You can also find a ministry God has called to minister to the poor and ask what you can do to help them. We recently sent someone from our ministry staff to all the shelters in our city to see which ones we felt would handle money responsibly if we gave them some. We found several very good people who were willing to do the work but needed money to do it.

If your church or the ministries you support are helping the poor, you are helping the poor also through them. Every church should be doing a lot of outreach to the lost and needy. God calls us to reach out to others, not to reach in, trying only to help ourselves. As we reach out to others, we are sowing seed, and God will bring a harvest to meet our personal needs.

I strongly encourage you to make giving a lifestyle. John Bunyan said, "You have not lived today until you have done something for someone who can never repay you."[20]

Greedy, stingy people are not only selfish; they are also more likely to compromise and act in dishonest ways in order to get more and more for themselves. For the greedy person, enough is never enough. The main word in their vocabulary is *more*. People who are never content with what they have will never be content even when they get what they want.

> If you are not content with what you have, you won't be content when you get what you want.

Be Generous on Purpose

Satan purposes to make us stingy and greedy. This is his goal, and he is relentless about accomplishing it. We should purpose to be generous and be relentless in doing it.

Let me encourage you to *plan your generosity*. Think of people you can help. Listen to what people tell you they like or need. Spend time with someone who is lonely. Practice random acts of kindness. Find out where the shelters for the poor are located in your city and donate money, clothing, blankets, socks, coats, or other items they need. It is fun to make a list of things you can do to be generous. Don't just follow my list; be creative and come up with your own ideas.

My goal is to give away something every day. It may be a generous tip at a restaurant, sending an encouraging note to someone, or cleaning out my closet and donating clothing. Or it may be being friendly toward someone I don't know. As I have said, there are countless ways to be a blessing to others. I don't reach my goal every day, but God knows I am willing if He puts something on my heart to do.

In addition to your regular giving, set aside an amount of money each month and start a giving fund. This could be a bank account or an envelope you keep at home. Keep some of the money from this fund with you at all times because you never know when an opportunity for generosity will present itself. If you are prepared, you won't miss it. Even if you can only begin with five dollars, that's a good place to start.

I keep a giving box in my closet, and when I come across items I no longer use, I put them in it. At any given time, the box may contain clothing, skin care products, decorating accessories I am replacing, shoes, purses, hair products, books I've finished or am not going to read, and candles I don't like the smell of. That box has had almost anything I can think of in it at some time or another. When it gets full, I give it to our daughter Laura, who distributes the contents to people she knows would use them and donates the rest to charities or thrift stores. At other times, I take the boxes to my office, and the items are given away to people there who would like to have them. We also have a church that is in a neighborhood where many people have needs, and we take things there for them to give away.

My generosity suggestions are, of course, based on how much you have. God doesn't expect you to give away everything you have, and you may not be in a position to do a lot, but do what you can do, because the worst thing we can do is nothing. How much stuff do you have in your house that you are not using or likely will never use? Your flesh may want to keep those items, "just in case," but if you did need them, you probably wouldn't remember where you left them, especially if you haven't used them in a long time.

When I do what I call de-junking my house, I find things I forgot I even had. Some of them are pleasant surprises, and I can use them, but others I look at and think, *Why did I ever buy this?*

Concerning money, there are two tests we must pass. One is how we act when we don't have enough, and the other is how we act when we have plenty. To pass the tests, we should trust God when we don't have enough and not complain. When we have plenty, we need to make sure we are not like the man I mentioned earlier in this chapter who had such a huge harvest that instead of using some to help others, he decided to tear down his barns and build bigger ones for himself, but never got the chance.

Because Galatians 6:7 (NIV) says "a man reaps what he sows," we will always reap a good harvest if we sow good seed. It may take some time, but it will happen. Of course, we also reap from bad seeds that we sow, so we want to use great wisdom with the thoughts we think, the words we speak, and the actions we take, because each of them is a seed.

Generosity and Gratitude

We can never outgive God. To illustrate this, let me tell you a story. Many years ago, I was about to sign a new contract with the first book publisher I had. The signing bonus would have been the largest sum of money Dave and I had ever received. I was so determined not to be greedy that I decided to give away all the money. I committed it to God before I even got it. In the meantime, my publisher had financial difficulties and decided to sell my contract and existing books to a better-known publisher, who offered me nine times as much as I had committed to give away. It was harvest time! Dave and I were able to give away what we had originally committed to give, and for the first time in our lives, to invest some money.

> You can never outgive God.

Whenever God blesses us, whether it is in a large way, such as what happened to me with the publishing contract, or in a way that involves less money, we should be thankful. I learned to be thankful for many small blessings, financial and otherwise, before I received such a remarkable experience with God's generosity.

It is my belief that the more grateful we are for what we have and what God has done for us, the more generous we will be to other people. As a matter of fact, being generous to others is one way we say thank You to the Lord. My regular morning prayer times include a lot of gratitude for all God has done for us and for all of our blessings. I have noticed that when I thank God and remember how He blesses me, I start wanting to do something to bless someone else.

When I am thankful, I am happy, and that makes me want to give to others.

You don't even have to wait for something good to happen to you before being a blessing to others; you can get the cycle started by aggressively giving first.

What Does Science Say about Gratitude?

Researchers have studied gratitude for two decades and discovered its value and benefits. Being thankful makes us happy, promotes better sleep, keeps us healthier, and makes us more generous.[21]

It is interesting that just in the last two decades, science has come to agree with what God has said all along.

PART 5

"It's Really Not About Me"

CHAPTER 17

For the Love of God

Anyone who loves me will obey my teaching. My Father will love them, and we will come to them and make our home with them. Anyone who does not love me will not obey my teaching. These words you hear are not my own; they belong to the Father who sent me.

John 14:23–24 NIV

We cannot be selfish and self-centered and walk in love at the same time. Since walking in love is the main commandment God wants us to obey, we need to give special attention to our love walk. When an expert in the law asked Jesus which of the commandments were most important, He replied:

> You shall love the Lord your God with all your heart and with all your soul and with all your mind (intellect). This is the great (most important, principal) and first commandment. And a second is like it: You shall love your neighbor as [you do] yourself. These two commandments sum up and upon them depend all the Law and the Prophets.
>
> Matthew 22:37–40

We must understand the importance Jesus places on loving God and loving people as we love ourselves. Here are two more scriptures that reinforce this point:

> The object and purpose of our instruction and charge is love, which springs from a pure heart and a good (clear) conscience and sincere (unfeigned) faith.
>
> 1 Timothy 1:5

> If you really fulfill the royal law according to the Scripture, "You shall love your neighbor as yourself," you are doing well.
>
> James 2:8 ESV

Since being selfish and self-centered prevents us from walking in love, we need to decide how we will obey God in this area. I could tell you to fight against selfishness all the time, but I think a better plan is to devote your energy to focusing on walking in love. If we are filled with God's love and let it flow through us to others, there will be no room for selfishness in our lives. It took me a long time to learn this lesson, and I struggled trying to conquer selfishness without making much progress until I realized that my focus should be on walking in love, which is positive, instead of fighting against selfishness, which is negative. Galatians 5:16 tells us to walk in the Spirit, and we will not fulfill the desires of the flesh. Focus on doing the right thing, and there will be no room in your life for the wrong thing.

> Focus on walking in love, not fighting against selfishness.

Receive God's Love and Give It Away

We love Him, because He first loved us.

1 John 4:19

It is so important for us to wholeheartedly understand that God loves us with His whole heart and that His love is in us. Romans 5:5 says that when we are born again, the love of God is poured into our hearts by the Holy Spirit. As you read this chapter, I encourage you to receive God's love as your own and learn to love yourself simply because God loves you. Then let that love flow through you to other people. Love everyone, even people who don't deserve it. Don't be stingy with God's love. Remind yourself that God loves you, and meditate on Scripture that tells you He does. Spend time in His presence receiving His love and purpose to express His love to others.

The Bible speaks often of walking in love. One of the many places it talks about this is in 2 John 5–6 (NIV):

> I am not writing you a new command but one we have had from the beginning. I ask that we love one another. And this is love: that we walk in obedience to his commands. As you have heard from the beginning, *his command is that you walk in love.* (emphasis mine)

> You have many opportunities to love people.

When we walk, we go one step at a time. To me, this means we will have many opportunities each day to love people. We will have many decisions to make and actions to take as we interact with those around us—and each one is a step in our love walk. We can love people with our thoughts, prayers, words, and actions.

Love and Sacrifice

Walking in love and sacrificing are inseparable. We may not have to sacrifice every time we show love, but many times we do have to surrender something we want in order to express love to someone else. I asked the Lord one time why more people don't walk in love, and I felt He showed me that this happens because love always costs something. It will cost time, energy, perhaps money, or something else. Remember that Jesus sacrificed Himself for us, so the sacrifices we make for others in obedience to Him are small prices to pay. Love is an effort, and since our flesh is lazy, people who are addicted to doing what they want to do will not walk in love.

Jesus endured the cross for the joy on the other side of it (Hebrews 12:2). If we will surrender our personal desires in order to follow the guidance of the Holy Spirit, we will experience great joy. Every sacrifice eventually has its reward. The reward may not come immediately, but it will come.

Paul writes that in order to share Christ's glory, we must share His sufferings. But he also notes that the suffering is nothing compared to the glory that will come (Romans 8:17–18). When you sacrifice to show love to someone, don't focus on what you are giving up; focus on what you will gain and the fact that you are obeying and pleasing God and bringing joy to someone else.

On several occasions, God has prompted me to give away some item, such as a piece of clothing or jewelry I really liked. Although parting with something I liked was difficult, I found joy in knowing I had been obedient to God and that what had belonged to me added joy to someone else's life. There are many ways to show love to people. Be friendly, compliment them, help meet a need in their life, pray for them, be patient with their weaknesses, and be quick to forgive them if they do something that hurts you. If you are aware that they struggle with some kind of sin, don't spread gossip; keep it to yourself and pray for them.

We show love more through how we treat people than through how we feel about them. You can show love to someone whom you don't particularly like. We don't have to feel like doing what is right in order to do it.

> *Show love to someone whom you don't particularly like.*

Loving Yourself

You cannot give away what you don't have. This is why Jesus says we are to love our neighbor as we love ourselves (Matthew 22:37–40). It is not wrong to love yourself. I like to say "Love yourself, but don't be *in love* with yourself." This means we are not to love ourselves in a self-centered way but to appreciate the fact that

God took special care when creating us and that Jesus thinks we are valuable enough for Him to suffer on the cross, take the punishment we deserve, and die in our place.

One of the biggest problems we face, and one reason people show so little love to one another, is that they lack love for themselves. It may sound strange that I am telling you to love yourself but not to be selfish. But you can love yourself and be unselfish if you love yourself with the love of God that has been poured into you by the Holy Spirit (Romans 5:5).

John, the Apostle of Love

The apostle John was originally known as one of the "Sons of Thunder," with his brother, James (Mark 3:17). But eventually, John became known as the apostle of love. This is very encouraging to me. God's love changes us, as it did John. Of all Jesus' disciples, John seemed to be the closest to Him. He referred to himself as the "disciple whom Jesus loved" (John 21:7, 20). He was not the only disciple Jesus loved, but He seemed to have an awareness of how much Jesus loved Him and to have an especially intimate relationship with our Lord. Here are some of John's statements about love:

> This is how we know who the children of God are and who the children of the devil are: Anyone who does not do what is right is not God's child, nor is anyone who does not love their brother and sister. For this is the message you heard from the beginning: We should love one another.
>
> 1 John 3:10–11 NIV

> We know that we have passed over out of death into Life by the fact that we love the brethren (our fellow

Christians). He who does not love abides (remains, is held and kept continually) in [spiritual] death.

1 John 3:14

This is how we know what love is: Jesus Christ laid down his life for us. And we ought to lay down our lives for our brothers and sisters.

1 John 3:16 NIV

But whoever has this world's goods, and sees his brother in need, and shuts up his heart from him, how does the love of God abide in him?

1 John 3:17 NKJV

Little children, let us not love [merely] in theory or in speech but in deed and in truth (in practice and in sincerity).

1 John 3:18

The Facets of Love

A facet is one side of something that is many-sided, such as a diamond. First Corinthians 13, often called the "love chapter" of the Bible, gives us a description of how love looks and what its facets are. I have heard that if a married couple would read these Scripture verses together each morning and live according to them, they would never get divorced.

First Corinthians 13:4–8 (NIV) describes love this way:

- Love is patient.
- Love is kind.
- Love does not envy.
- Love does not boast.

- Love is not proud.
- Love does not dishonor others.
- Love is not self-seeking.
- Love is not easily angered.
- Love keeps no record of wrongs.
- Love does not delight in evil but rejoices with the truth.
- Love always protects.
- Love always believes the best of everyone.
- Love always hopes.
- Love always perseveres.
- Love never fails.

I recommend that instead of simply reading this list, you study each of these words. Look up their definition and search God's Word for other scriptures that help you understand them. Meditate on them and ask yourself daily if you are operating in these facets of love. I think this exercise could help keep all of us on the right path.

Love, Faith, and Forgiveness Work Together

Galatians 5:6 tells us that faith works through and is energized by love. We see this principle expressed also in Mark 11:24–25:

> For this reason I am telling you, whatever you ask for in prayer, believe (trust and be confident) that it is granted to you, and you will [get it]. And whenever you stand praying, if you have anything against anyone, forgive him and let it drop (leave it, let it go), in order that your Father Who is in heaven may also forgive you your [own] failings and shortcomings and let them drop.

How often do you ask God to do some-
thing for you while simultaneously being
angry with someone who has hurt or
offended you? These scriptures say plainly

> *When you pray, you must also forgive.*

that when we pray, we must also forgive. Mark 11:26 goes on to
say that if we don't forgive others, God won't forgive us.

It is important for us to take this Scripture passage seriously. I
know from years of Bible teaching that many Christians are angry
with someone they refuse to forgive. They think they are justified
in their anger because the person who hurt them doesn't deserve
forgiveness. Then they don't understand why their prayers are not
being answered.

God's Word tells us to love our enemies, help them if they are
in need, pray for them, and bless them, not curse them (Luke
6:27–28, 35; Romans 12:14). Not one of us deserves God's forgive-
ness, but God gives it, and we gladly receive it. Let's treat others
the way He treats us.

We Must Master Anger

People who are angry cannot walk in love. They are too busy being
upset about everything they don't like that happens to them. They
become angry when they don't get their way, and they hold on to
their anger without giving thought to the negative ways it affects
them personally.

In our society today, I believe more people
are angry than are at peace. I can person-
ally testify that anger is an emotion that will
make you sick if you allow it to continue.

> *Life is too short to spend it angry.*

It causes stress, and stress causes disease.[22] Life is too short to
spend it angry. Why be angry with someone who is enjoying their
life and doesn't even care that you are upset?

You may be thinking about a situation that makes you angry right now, wanting to say, "But Joyce, you just don't understand what has happened to me!" Everyone must deal with circumstances they don't like at times. Life is filled with circumstances we do not like, but they should not control us. The Holy Spirit should control us as we willingly surrender to His guidance. Let Him teach you how to control yourself, and do not allow your circumstances to dictate your emotions or behavior. In the prayers Paul writes in his epistles, he does not ask God to remove believers' problems. He prays that they will be able to handle whatever comes their way with good temper. For example, he prays in Colossians 1:11: "[We pray] that you may be invigorated and strengthened with all power according to the might of His glory, [to exercise] every kind of endurance and patience (perseverance and forbearance) with joy."

I spent years angry about conditions I didn't like in my life and kept wanting them to change. I finally realized that even if those unpleasant circumstances did change, before long something else I didn't like would come along. I finally decided that I needed to learn to be content no matter what my circumstances were. I was willing to change if God would help me. This decision was life-changing for me. An important part of spiritual maturity is the ability to be in the midst of a circumstance you don't like and trust God to deal with it while you continue to enjoy your life and love others.

Jesus said as He hung on the cross, "Father, forgive them, for they know not what they do" (Luke 23:34). There are several schools of thought concerning who "them" and "they" refer to. I believe He was talking about the people who nailed Him to the cross and those who supported His crucifixion, in addition to the thieves hanging on each side of Him. I also believe He was concerned about the spiritual damage they had done to themselves.

When people hurt you, they are hurting themselves more than they are hurting you. Pray for them and ask God to forgive them, just as Jesus forgives them.

Anger is rooted in selfishness and pride. According to James 1:20, human anger "does not promote the righteousness God [wishes and requires]" for us. And Proverbs 29:11 says, "A [self-confident] fool utters all his anger, but a wise man holds it back and stills it." In addition, we read in Ecclesiastes 7:9, "Do not be quick in spirit to be angry or vexed, for anger and vexation lodge in the bosom of fools."

A Christian's attitude should be one of meekness, not arrogance and anger. Jesus is humble, meek, and lowly, and we should take His yoke on us and learn to be like He is (Matthew 11:28–30). As children of God, we should operate in self-control.

Paul teaches us that when we feel angry, we must not sin (Ephesians 4:26). Anger is a natural response to an injustice, and forgiveness is a supernatural response. We can forgive because God gives us grace and strength to do so.

Anger and Pride

People who are selfish and angry don't like not getting what they want. They have not developed the ability to hear the word *no* and remain joyful, because they are filled with pride. They often have an opinion on every subject, and they consider their thoughts and convictions infallible. They insist on seeing other people adopt their ideas. They lose their tempers because they deem themselves extraordinary and view themselves as superior. In short, people who think and act as I have described are proud. If they get rid of their pride, they will also get rid of their hot tempers.

Someone who had a quick temper once told me that he had learned that being right is highly overrated. How often do we become angry simply because we argue to be right in a conversation or disagreement? It's just not worth it. Why do we care so much about who is right? God knows, and if we need to be proven to be right, He can arrange for it.

People who are proud and angry can pick their pain. They can have the pain of never changing and remaining the same for the rest of their life, or they can choose the pain of changing. The pain of never changing lasts a lifetime, but the pain of change is short-lived, and the reward is joy and peace.

> *The pain of change is short-lived, but the pain of never changing lasts a lifetime.*

Pride blames others because taking responsibility would require humility. We must stop blaming others for our anger or we will never be free. Even if someone is not treating us well, it doesn't relieve us of our responsibility before God to do what is right.

Love is the most important and most excellent thing in the world. I encourage you to receive God's love and then give it away every way you can. As you seek to walk in love, your selfishness will decrease and your joy and power will increase.

CHAPTER 18

What About Me?

And Jesus called [to Him] the throng with His disciples and said to them, If anyone intends to come after Me, let him deny himself [forget, ignore, disown, and lose sight of himself and his own interests] and take up his cross, and [joining Me as a disciple and siding with My party] follow with Me [continually, cleaving steadfastly to Me].

Mark 8:34

For quite a few years, whenever I read Mark 8:34, my first thought was *If I do what this verse says, then what about me? Who will take care of me?* I felt that if I obeyed this biblical teaching, I would never get anything I wanted, and I simply wasn't willing to live that way.

But, as I grew in my relationship with God and fell more and more in love with Jesus, I finally wanted to obey this scripture. I learned that if I stopped trying to take care of myself and surrendered all to the Lord, He would take care of me. The scripture below is God's promise to take care of us if we stop trying to do it ourselves by persistently worrying about what will happen to us.

> Casting the whole of your care [all your anxieties, all your worries, all your concerns, once and for all] on Him, for He cares for you affectionately and cares about you watchfully.
>
> 1 Peter 5:7

God does a much better job of taking care of us than we could ever do taking care of ourselves, and He will do special and surprisingly good things for us. There are also times when He may allow us to go through difficult situations, and "What about me?" will rise up in our thinking again. But these testing times are actually good for us, and eventually we will see that what we thought was our worst enemy turned out to be our best friend, simply because it is the hard times in our lives that bring us closer to God and help us grow spiritually. Selfishness doesn't go without determination, and we need to learn that God's way is always better than ours. But it usually takes several rounds of testing before we are ready to give in.

God takes care of you better than you can take care of yourself.

Paul experienced many extreme difficulties, but each of them brought him closer to the Lord and taught him to trust God completely. Consider his words in 2 Corinthians 4:8–10:

> We are hedged in (pressed) on every side [troubled and oppressed in every way], but not cramped or crushed; we suffer embarrassments and are perplexed and unable to find a way out, but not driven to despair; we are pursued (persecuted and hard driven), but not deserted [to stand alone]; we are struck down to the ground, but never struck out and destroyed; always carrying about in the body the liability and exposure to the same putting to death that the Lord Jesus suffered, so that the [resurrection] life of Jesus also may be shown forth by and in our bodies.

It sounds as though Paul and his companions experienced every kind of trouble. But they never gave up. No matter what they went through, they knew they were never alone and that Jesus was always with them. They were willing to die to self so the resurrection power of Christ might be shown through them.

Another example of extreme difficulty in Paul's life is found in 2 Corinthians 1:8–9:

> For we do not want you to be uninformed, brethren, about the affliction and oppressing distress which befell us in [the province of] Asia, how we were so utterly and unbearably weighed down and crushed that we

despaired even of life [itself]. Indeed, we felt within our-
selves that we had received the [very] sentence of death,
but that was to keep us from trusting in and depending
on ourselves instead of on God Who raises the dead.

These scriptures and others like them have gotten me through
many tough days. I didn't want to depend on myself, but on God.
However, like Paul, I had to be tested. We never know for sure
what we will do, how we will behave, or even what we truly
believe unless we are tested. Initially, these tests tend to bring out
of us ugly, fleshly behavior, but eventually, as the self dies and is
replaced by love and trusting God, we see the nature of Christ ris-
ing up to meet these challenges.

Are you ready to surrender your selfish "What about me?" atti-
tude and trust God to take care of you? If
so, then pray this prayer: "Father, I surren-
der all to You, and I trust You to take care
of me."

Father, I surrender all to You.

George Müller said, "The beginning of anxiety is the end of
faith, and the beginning of true faith is the end of anxiety."[23]

First Peter 5:7 teaches us to cast (meaning to throw) all of our
care on God. This is an invitation to trust God with ourselves
and everything that concerns us. In response, we will see Him do
amazing things in our lives.

Trust God and learn how to enter His rest.

As we trust God, we will learn how to
enter His rest. His rest is not a rest *from*
work; it does not refer to taking a nap
or getting a good night's sleep. His Sab-
bath rest is a rest we enter *while* we work. It is not the absence of
troubles or difficulties, but being at peace in the midst of them,
knowing that God will take care of them—and of us—in His own
special way and timing. It is refreshing to know that we can have

a problem and enjoy our life at the same time because we trust God.

Noah Webster's 1828 Dictionary defines *trust* as: "Confidence; a reliance or resting of the mind on the integrity, veracity, justice, friendship or other sound principle of another person."[24] The word *rest* is the Greek word *anapauó*, which means "to give rest, refresh, to give oneself rest, to take rest; to keep quiet, of calm and patient expectation."[25] If we enter the rest of God, we can be refreshed while we work or wait for God to solve a problem for us. Physical work may make us tired physically, but mental and emotional distress brings a tormenting type of tiredness that no amount of physical rest can cure. Only inner peace, freedom from worry and anxiety, and trusting God can give us the type of supernatural rest God wants us to have.

To trust God is to release a burden or a heavy weight we are carrying. I frequently speak with people who tell me how much they are trusting God. In the same conversation, they also tell me how worried, fearful, and stressed they are. They may be *trying* to trust God, but they have not arrived yet. I think we all begin this way and gradually develop true trust in God.

If you want to trust God but still find yourself stressed and anxious instead of at rest, just be honest with Him. If you are trying to trust Him but just haven't gotten there yet, tell Him and ask Him to help you. There's no point in trying to pretend with God, because He always knows the truth behind our actions.

There is a story in the Bible about a man who wanted Jesus to heal his son. When Jesus asked the man if he believed He could heal the boy, he was honest and said, " 'Lord, I believe; help my unbelief!' " (Mark 9:24 NKJV). His son was healed. We don't always have to have perfect faith in order for God to work in our lives; we simply need to be honest with God.

Trust is based on what we know about the character of the

> Trust is based on what you know about another's character.

person we trust. Study God's character and you will discover that He is good, kind, loving, generous, just, holy, and faithful and has many more wonderful qualities. He is also all-knowing, all-seeing, and always present everywhere. We cannot do things behind closed doors and think God doesn't know about them.

Faith Is Required

Living a lifestyle of casting our care on God and trusting Him requires faith. My definition of faith, based on Hebrews 11:1, is that it is the evidence of things we cannot see and the proof of their reality. It is the assurance and belief that God loves and cares for you, and because He does, that He will do marvelous things in your life as you trust and wait on Him.

Peter wanted to walk on water with Jesus, but he had to first get out of the boat (Matthew 14:22–33). Just imagine how hard that first step must have been. He did walk on the water until he lost his focus on Jesus and began to focus on the waves around him. At that point he began to sink, but Jesus reached out and took hold of him so he did not drown. Likewise, when we step out to walk in faith, we may not do it perfectly, but Jesus will always be there to help us through our weaknesses and give us an opportunity to begin again. Thankfully, God's mercies are new every morning (Lamentations 3:22–23).

When I quit my job to study and prepare for a teaching ministry that had not become a reality, I did it in faith, but my knees

> Faith is moving forward even though you are afraid.

were shaking with fear. Faith is not the absence of fear; it is often moving forward while you still feel afraid. I just kept moving in the direction I felt God was leading, and many times I had to "do it afraid." But God proved Himself faithful to me over and over again. Dave and I never had a bill go unpaid, and when we needed things we had no money to buy, we learned how to trust God for them. His methods of provision were often unique and varied, but also wonderful.

Faith requires waiting with no evidence that God is doing anything at all. This is the test of faith we must all go through. When we have no experience living this way, it is nerve-racking, but each time we experience God's faithfulness, it is easier

> *Faith means waiting with no evidence that God is doing anything at all.*

to trust Him the next time. When I think back on all the time I wasted in worry and fear, I wish I had known then what I know now. But the only way we can get that kind of experience is to go through the tests and learn how to pass them. Being able to trust God completely is the most wonderful thing I can think of. It is the only way we can remain joyful and content in all seasons of life.

God promises in His Word to take care of us. These promises are so many that I couldn't possibly quote them all, but here are a few that will encourage you:

> Delight yourself in the Lord, and he will give you the desires of your heart.
>
> Psalm 37:4 ESV

> The Lord is my shepherd; I shall not want.
>
> Psalm 23:1 NKJV

> Seek the Kingdom of God above all else, and live righteously, and he will give you everything you need.
>
> Matthew 6:33 NLT

And my God shall supply all your need according to His
riches in glory by Christ Jesus.

Philippians 4:19 NKJV

He who did not spare his own Son, but gave him up for
us all—how will he not also, along with him, graciously
give us all things?

Romans 8:32 NIV

I would not have made it through the testing times had I not
turned to these scriptures, and many others like them, over and
over again, and let them calm my anxious soul.

"Faith comes by hearing, and hearing by the word of God"
(Romans 10:17 NKJV). The more you study God's Word and act on
it, the more your faith will grow. Speak the Word with your own
mouth and listen to others teach it. As you hear it, your faith will
become strong. You have to use the little faith you have in order to
grow and keep growing until you have great faith. Jesus said that
even faith the size of a mustard seed (which is one of the tiniest
seeds on earth) can move mountains (Matthew 17:20). You are
capable of great things through Christ, but it requires dying to
self and putting all your faith in the Lord.

What If I Don't Get What I Want?

The fear of not getting what we want is the root of our reluctance
to trust God completely. But if we are trusting God with our lives
and don't get what we want, we should continue trusting that He
loves us and has our best interests in His heart. We also need to
trust that if we don't get what we are hoping for, He has something
better in mind for us.

You may find this difficult to agree with, but sometimes it is better for us not to get what we want and learn to be content anyway. The fact that you don't get what you want when you want it doesn't mean you won't get it

> *Learn to be content though you may not get what you want.*

eventually. It could be right for you at some point—just not right now. If you have children, I imagine that at some time you have told them "It isn't good for you to always get your way and get everything you want." We want our children to be able to hear the word *no* and still trust us, and God wants the same from us.

Because I grew up in an abusive home surrounded by selfish people who never really took care of me, I had a very hard time as an adult learning to trust people and to trust God. I always had to take care of myself, and before I learned to trust, I often hurt Dave's feelings because of my lack of trust in him. But I simply was not convinced that he or anyone else would make a decision for me that wasn't selfish on their part. I knew he loved me, but my parents had told me they loved me and then didn't take proper care of me. Therefore, the words *I love you* didn't mean much to me. It took years of experience with Dave for me to finally get to where I could trust him to make decisions for me and believe he truly did have my best interests in his heart. I saw his love through his sacrifice. He sacrificed his desires and allowed me to be in full-time ministry. Not only did he allow me to follow that path, but he has followed it with me and has been by my side every step of the way. God blessed me with the best husband in the world, and it was through watching him that I learned what love looks like. Words are nice, but loving actions are what really make us feel loved.

Trusting God does not guarantee we will get what we want, but it does guarantee that we will get what is best for us at the right time. Can you trust that God's will is better than yours? Learn to *relax* and let God be God in your life. Give Him a chance, and He will prove His faithfulness to you.

Trusting God means living by faith, and it is a daily decision. The children of Israel had to trust God for their manna one day at a time (Exodus 16:4, 21). Ashleigh Brilliant said, "I try to take one day at a time, but sometimes several days attack me at once."[26] I know how this feels, and I'm sure you do, too. Self-reliance is foolish because we usually think more highly of ourselves than we ought to (Romans 12:3). When people are asked to do a job, I don't like to hear them say "Oh, that's a piece of cake," meaning that it will be easy. They are basically saying "I can do that with no problem." But if they don't rely on God, they more than likely will have problems.

> Trust that God's will is better than yours.

It honors God when we rely on Him in little things as well as big things. "Help me, Lord" is a prayer we should pray often throughout each day. Although it is simple, it is one of the most powerful prayers we can pray.

CHAPTER 19

Resurrection Power

Behold! I have given you authority and power to trample upon serpents and scorpions, and [physical and mental strength and ability] over all the power that the enemy [possesses]; and nothing shall in any way harm you.

Luke 10:19

God wants us to be spiritually powerful, not weak. He has given us power and authority, according to Luke 10:19, but we can do things that will either weaken or block that power. Paul prays in Ephesians 3:16 that we will be strengthened in our inner being through the Holy Spirit. Physical muscle and strength are certainly beneficial and healthy, but spiritual power is what enables us to walk through this life as Jesus would have us walk.

Living a life of sacrifice and love is not simply something we decide to do; we need God's strength and power to enable us.

Consider a portion of Paul's prayer in Philippians 3:10 (AMP):

> And this, so that I may know Him [experientially, becoming more thoroughly acquainted with Him, understanding the remarkable wonders of His Person more completely] and [in the same way experience] the power of His resurrection [which overflows and is active in believers].

I want to be lifted above the things the devil designs to make us miserable in life. I want to know the power of Christ's resurrection also; don't you? When we know this, no matter what uncomfortable or unfair situation is happening around us, we can rise above it and continue enjoying God and life while we wait on Him to deliver or vindicate us.

I think it's fair to say that much of what goes on in everyday life in the world is full of darkness and death (every kind of misery), bringing unhappiness and dissatisfaction. But there is a place we can live in Christ that lifts us above every influence of that misery, even though we live in the midst of it. In simple terms, this

means we can live powerfully in this world
and be peaceful and joyful, no matter what
is going on around us. To enjoy this kind of
life, we must live close to God and remain
in continual fellowship with Him. *Con-*
tinual doesn't mean every second of every day, for that would be
impossible, but it does mean on a regular basis throughout each
day. In ourselves without Jesus we are weak, but in Him we are
powerful.

> *You can be peaceful*
> *and joyful, no matter*
> *what is going on*
> *around you.*

Second Corinthians 13:4 says, "For though He was crucified
in weakness, yet He goes on living by the power of God. And
though we too are weak in Him [as He was humanly weak], yet
in dealing with you [we shall show ourselves] alive and strong in
[fellowship with] Him by the power of God." And Romans 8:11
says that if the same Spirit that raised Christ from the dead dwells
in us, it will give life to our mortal bodies. In the King James Ver-
sion of the Bible, the phrase *give life* is rendered *quicken*, which
means "to make alive."[27] It also means "to give or restore vigor or
activity to; stir up, rouse, or stimulate."[28]

As believers, we are children of God, so His Spirit does dwell in
us (1 Corinthians 3:16). To me, this means a steady flow of resur-
rection power courses through me all the time if I will believe it and
receive it. This is one reason it is so important to stay connected to
God. Think of it this way: If a lamp is plugged into the wall and I
unplug it, then it will lose power immediately. But the power can
be restored just as quickly if I plug it back in. Stay plugged into
God, and if you get unplugged, just plug back in again.

Stopped-Up Wells

Jesus stood and called out [in a loud voice], "If anyone is
thirsty, let him come to Me and drink! He who believes

in Me [who adheres to, trusts in, and relies on Me], as
the Scripture has said, 'From his innermost being will
flow continually rivers of living water.'"

John 7:37–38 AMP

From this Scripture passage we can see that Jesus wants a con-
tinual flow of power coming from within us. This power will keep
us happy and have a positive effect on the people around us. But a
blockage will hinder its flow.

Have you ever had a pipe that only gave you a trickle of water?
You put up with it for a while but eventually call a plumber who
uses equipment to look into the pipe and find the problem. He
normally finds something blocking the flow. Often, someone has
put something in the sink that didn't belong there, and instead of
moving through the pipe to the sewer, it got clogged and needed
to be removed.

In the Old Testament, one way the Philistines fought against the
Israelites was to stop up their wells. They filled them with earth
and stones so no one could get water from them. To use this as
an example of how the devil fights against us, we can say that he
tries to stop up our wells (spirits) with dirt (the world) and stones
of various types. These may be stones of offense, unforgiveness,
sin, selfishness, disobedience, jealousy, envy, pride, negative expe-
riences, or other undesirable things. Just as Isaac opened the wells
Abraham dug and the Philistines stopped up (Genesis 26:18), Jesus
came to open our wells so living water can once again flow from us.

If we remain strong spiritually, we keep the negative influences
of the world out of our lives. But spiritually weak people give in to
peer pressure. They compromise and try to serve God, while not
being fully committed to Him. Their power is diluted; their well
(spirit) is stopped up. They are what Jesus refers to in Revelation
3:16 as "lukewarm."

Being selfish and self-centered will definitely stop up your well, but through repentance and a willingness to change, the power of love can flow once again, and many people can be brought to faith in Christ through the living water that flows from you.

> Love is the most powerful force in the world.

Selfishness renders us weak, but love is the most powerful force in the world.

Helping Others Helps You Deal with Your Problems

Consider this remarkable story about Donna and her marriage. Her story is proof that forgetting yourself and helping others is the best way to overcome your own problems.

I was married and had a great relationship with God. Seventeen years into the marriage, my husband had an affair. It wrecked me, and I couldn't get my mind off of it. For weeks all I could think about were the problems in my marriage, and I prayed to God, saying, "I can't go through this every day." I was floundering, I was getting depressed, and I had to do something to move past the pain.

God led me to volunteer at an adult day care. The first time I walked in there, my first thought was that I couldn't stand the smell, but then I looked at the people. These were disabled people who couldn't take care of themselves. I remember a man with diabetes who lost his eyesight and his leg to the disease. I would just sit and talk with him to make him smile. There was a young man, twenty-seven years old, who had been shot in the head and lost his ability to walk. He loved to make me laugh, so I also spent time with him.

These people's problems were greater than mine. They were living in family members' homes and had nowhere to go but to an adult day care every day. I had the opportunity to entertain them with games, do their nails, listen to them, talk to them, anything to make them feel human.

Volunteering at the day care stopped me from daily replaying the negative thoughts in my head about my marriage. Because of that, I could deal with my problems. Eventually, my marriage healed. I realized that I had placed my husband on a pedestal higher than God. The struggle I went through helped me put things back into proper perspective. This happened twenty-two years ago, and now we've been married for nearly forty years. I could not have dealt with my marital problems had I done nothing but focus on myself and my pain.

Today my husband and I sponsor the building of water wells in poverty-stricken areas that need clean water. Knowing we're doing something in the world to meet a need that God wants us to meet has given us great purpose. Getting our minds off ourselves helps us and the people who are benefiting from what we can do for them.

Disobedience

I am so glad Donna obeyed the leading of the Holy Spirit. Wherever He leads us, He has blessings in store for us. We don't obey Him simply to receive blessings; we obey Him because we love Him and want to please Him, but we end up being blessed because God is good.

Any kind of disobedience is like a stone the devil throws down your well (spirit), and the river of life won't flow until the disobedience is removed. Isaiah spoke a word from God to the Israelites: "Oh, that you had hearkened to My commandments! Then your peace and prosperity would have been like a flowing river, and your righteousness [the holiness and purity of the nation] like the [abundant] waves of the sea" (Isaiah 48:18).

Obedience to God brings rivers of peace and waves of righteousness. When we are obedient, God defeats our enemies for us. God says in Exodus 23:22, "But if you will indeed listen to and obey His voice and all that I speak, then I will be an enemy to your enemies and an adversary to your adversaries."

I want God to be an enemy to my enemies, don't you? We should be on guard and pray that we recognize the devil's tactics and resist him before he stops up our power. Thankfully, because of God's grace and forgiveness, we can unstop our wells through sincere repentance. After forty-six years of teaching God's Word, I know how important it is for me to not only be filled with God's power, but to make sure I live my life in such a way that the power of God can flow through me to break the bondages in people's lives and heal their brokenness.

If you want to keep the power of the Holy Spirit flowing like rivers of living water from your life, then you will need to be vigilant and committed to obeying God. This requires more than one sacrifice; it requires a lifetime of sacrifices, because we cannot just do what we want, think, and feel. We must move past living only for our self-interests and do God's will, knowing that His ways are always better than ours.

If you are born again, you have the power of the Holy Spirit in you. But multitudes of Christians know nothing about the power that is ours. I was in church regularly for years and never once heard that I had the power of the Holy Spirit in me. I was told to resist sin, but I tried to do it in

> If you are born again, you have the power of the Holy Spirit in you.

the strength of my flesh, rather than relying on the power of God in me. We can't make use of something we don't know we have. According to Ephesians 1:3, we have "every spiritual...blessing in the heavenly realm." The amplification of the verse says these blessings are given by the Holy Spirit, but they do us no good if we are not aware that we have them. Acts 1:8 informs us further about the power God has given us:

> But you shall receive power (ability, efficiency, and might) when the Holy Spirit has come upon you, and you shall be My witnesses in Jerusalem and all Judea and Samaria and to the ends (the very bounds) of the earth.

If you haven't already asked God to fill you with the Holy Spirit, do so. Then start believing His power is in you, and because of this, you can do things you would not ordinarily be able to do. When you receive Christ as your Savior and are born again, you receive the Holy Spirit. But to be filled with the Holy Spirit requires making room for Him in every area of your life. When you do this, you will be able to do things you could never do on your own:

- You can go through difficult situations and still walk in the fruit of the Holy Spirit, trust God, and love people.
- You can resist any kind of temptation because God will never allow you to be tempted beyond what you can bear (1 Corinthians 10:13).
- You can live a surrendered life and be content and joyful.
- You can live totally free from unforgiveness and offense because when people hurt you, you are more concerned about what they are doing to themselves than what they are doing to you. When Jesus was being crucified, He said,

"Father, forgive them, for they know not what they do" (Luke 23:34).

- You can live unselfishly, sacrificially, and not think *What about me?*
- You can enter God's rest and enjoy life even if your circumstances are difficult.

Living with God's power is wonderful. It is like someone who has lived in the dark all their life suddenly discovers they have electricity in their house and turns on the lights. God's power has been available to you all the time, but if you have never accessed it, now is the time to begin.

Power, Love, and a Sound Mind

Second Timothy 1:7 says, "For God has not given us a spirit of fear, but of power and of love and of a sound mind" (NKJV). This is a wonderful scripture that gives us tremendous hope. Fear is our archenemy. Satan tries to use fear as often as he can to stop us from doing what God wants us to do. But we don't have a spirit of fear, but of power. Some Bible translations say we have "self-discipline" (NIV) or "self-control" (ESV) instead of "a sound mind." Either way, we have:

- Power toward the enemy
- Love toward other people
- Self-control toward ourselves

What Do You Believe about Yourself?

Most people believe negative things about themselves and think it would be wrong to believe anything good about themselves. Some don't think there is anything positive to believe about themselves, and some believe that having positive thoughts about themselves would represent pride and go against Romans 12:3, which teaches us not to think of ourselves more highly than we ought.

But Scripture also teaches us to acknowledge every good thing that is in us:

> That the sharing of your faith may become effective by the acknowledgment of every good thing which is in you in Christ Jesus.
>
> Philemon 6 NKJV

The goodness in us is not our own; it is what Jesus has deposited in us. It comes from His presence in us. Instead of denying it or assuming some kind of false humility, we should understand who and what God has made us to be in Jesus and start living up to it. You will never become anything that you don't believe you are. Let me ask you:

- Do you believe you can do anything you need to do through Christ who strengthens you? (Philippians 4:13)
- Do you believe God hears and answers your prayers? (Mark 11:24)
- Do you believe God loves you unconditionally and has a good plan for your life? (Jeremiah 29:11; 1 John 4:16)
- Do you believe you are the head and not the tail, above and not beneath? (Deuteronomy 28:13; Ephesians 1:18–23)
- Do you believe God has forgiven and forgotten your sins? (Isaiah 43:25; Ephesians 1:7)
- Do you have the confidence to step out and try new things without fearing failure? (Isaiah 41:10)

The Bible is filled with truth concerning the good things about you and the blessings God has for you, but in order to access them you must believe them. The devil will lie to you and try to deceive you to prevent you from believing and receiving good things, but you must decide if you believe God's Word more than you believe the devil's lies. When you decide to believe God's Word no matter how you feel, what you want, what you think, or how your circumstances look, you are on your way to a successful, powerful, wonderful life.

Life won't always be easy. In fact, Jesus promises that we will face difficulty, but He also says we can cheer up because He has overcome the world (John 16:33). It is useless to believe you will never face challenges or trouble, but you can choose to believe you can live above it and that, no matter what it is, God will always take care of you.

Power Belongs to You

God's power belongs to you, and you need to see yourself as powerful, able, capable, and qualified. You will never go beyond what you believe about yourself. You are strong in the Lord and the power of His might (Ephesians 6:10 NKJV). What kind of life do you want to have? If you want a good one, then you must begin believing what God says about you. You may not feel powerful,

> You need to see yourself as powerful, because God's power belongs to you.

but you are. If you start believing you are powerful, your feelings will catch up with your believing. Say aloud several times each day, "God's power is in me. I am strong in the Lord, and I can do whatever I need to do in life through Christ."

CHAPTER 20

This Hurts!

The saying is sure and worthy of confidence: If we have died with Him, we shall also live with Him.

2 Timothy 2:11

Any teenager will tell you that it hurts to grow up. The process of maturing requires taking responsibility for things one's parents have taken care of previously—such as getting a job to make money and dealing with the consequences of decisions. Teenagers want to make their own decisions, and parents eventually must let them do so, but parents should also let their teens deal with the consequences of any bad decisions they make. This is the only way they will learn to think seriously before they act. We all want to be rescued—we even want God to rescue us. But being rescued is not always best for us long term. If I cleaned up every mess one of my children made when they were young, they would have never stopped making messes. But after they cleaned up a few themselves, they learned to think twice before making another one.

Likewise, it is also painful to grow up spiritually. We begin our life with God as baby Christians, and God allows us to remain that way for a period of time. I call this the honeymoon phase of our relationship with God. We feel loved; our prayers seem to be answered quickly; God provides for us miraculously; we may be instantly set free from some kind of bondage; we are happy and peaceful, and everything seems wonderful. Of course, we would love for this to continue, but it eventually comes to a halt, and we usually don't understand why. We may think we have done something wrong, but the change simply means it's time to start our classes in spiritual maturity.

At this point we begin learning that we can no longer live according to what we want, what we think, and how we feel. It is time to begin surrendering to God. But if we are self-willed or stubborn, this will take a long time; and the longer it takes, the more it hurts. Believe it or not, surrendering to God is much easier than stubbornly holding on to what He wants us to let go of.

I believe cooperating with what God is doing in our lives is much easier if we understand it, and that is one reason I wrote this book. I believe this subject is woefully neglected by many Bible teachers and preachers, but it is very important. Why is it neglected? Maybe the teachers don't understand it themselves, or maybe they don't teach it because it isn't a subject that excites their audience, even though it will help them immensely in their walk with God.

In Acts 20:1 we read that Paul called for the disciples and "warned and consoled and urged and encouraged them." In Acts 20:20 we read that he did not shrink from telling them anything that was for their benefit. And in Acts 20:27, he writes that he "never shrank or kept back or fell short from declaring" to them "the whole purpose and plan and counsel of God."

It is dangerous to preach and teach only the aspects of the gospel that make people feel good, such as the love and mercy of God, His forgiveness, His patience, His kindness, and His provision. We must also teach about His correction and chastisement and the need for spiritual growth and holiness. Appreciate your pastors and teachers when they are bold enough to teach you the parts of the gospel that may correct or warn you just as much as you appreciate them when they teach the parts that encourage you.

Death Brings Life

When we die physically and go to heaven, we will be introduced to a life that is wonderful beyond anything we can imagine. Dying to self is much the same way. If we have died with Christ, we shall live with Him (2 Timothy 2:11). Dying to self means dying to our

> *Dying to self means dying to our way and accepting God's way.*

way and accepting God's way. It means dying to what we want if what we want doesn't agree with God's will for us.

We must consider our flesh dead to sin in order to live for Christ. According to Scripture, we died with Jesus when He died, and we were raised to a new life when He was raised (2 Timothy 2:11), but we must view this as a fact and believe it. We die to the desire to sin and no longer want to sin. We are dead to it! That death brings life, a better life than we have ever known. However, there is a problem. Although our new nature is dead to sin, our flesh is still very much alive, and it fights our new desire not to sin. As Jesus says, "the spirit indeed is willing, but the flesh is weak" (Matthew 26:41).

I never considered selfishness to be a sin until God showed me that it is. I was living a low life, but it was the only type of life I had known, and I didn't realize it was so far below what God wanted for me. Only after I began to change and truly care for others and want God's will more than my own did I begin to live a higher and much better life. I was sacrificing external things, yet in my spirit I was more joyful than ever before. Without realizing it, I had been clinging to what made me unhappy. I thought the way to happiness, contentment, and peace was getting everything I wanted and getting it my way. I was wrong!

I learned to view the pain I felt when letting go of things that were no longer suitable for me as something positive. It hurt to give them up, but I also knew that it meant I was growing closer to God and His will for me. I knew the pain I felt in my soul was actually birthing life in me.

Dying to what I wanted was very difficult and painful in the beginning, but the final outcome was that it "hurt good." I came to actually enjoy the pain because I knew it was taking me to a better place.

I have been working out with a trainer for many years, so I rarely get sore. But recently I worked out by myself and did something new, and I was sore for three days. Although it hurt, I was a little excited because I knew it meant that I had used a muscle that wasn't being used previously, and I knew the pain meant gain in that area.

"Self" is a fact of life. We have to deal with it until we are no longer on this earth. I pray every day that God will help me not to be selfish, because without His help I am still inclined in that direction. This is not a once-in-a-lifetime prayer, but a daily one. Spiritual maturity is an ongoing process that lasts to some degree until we leave the earth, so just get used to it and realize that when it hurts, something is getting better.

Work Out Your Salvation

We can never work for our salvation because it is a gift of God's grace, and we receive it through faith. Consider Ephesians 2:8–9:

> For it is by free grace (God's unmerited favor) that you are saved (delivered from judgment and made partakers of Christ's salvation) through [your] faith. And this [salvation] is not of yourselves [of your own doing, it came not through your own striving], but it is the gift of God; not because of works [not the fulfillment of the Law's demands], lest any man should boast. [It is not the result of what anyone can possibly do, so no one can pride himself in it or take glory to himself.

This passage makes clear that we cannot earn our salvation. But the next one I will show you says we should "work out" our own salvation. It doesn't say "work for" but "work out," and understanding the difference is very important:

Therefore, my dear ones, as you have always obeyed [my suggestions], so now, not only [with the enthusiasm you would show] in my presence but much more because I am absent, work out (cultivate, carry out to the goal, and fully complete) your own salvation with reverence and awe and trembling (self-distrust, with serious caution, tenderness of conscience, watchfulness against temptation, timidly shrinking from whatever might offend God and discredit the name of Christ). [Not in your own strength] for it is God Who is all the while effectually at work in you [energizing and creating in you the power and desire], both to will and to work for His good pleasure and satisfaction and delight.

Philippians 2:12–13

With the Holy Spirit's help (not in our own strength), we must work out what God has worked in us by His grace. When we are

> You must work out what God has worked in you.

born again, God makes us holy in our spirit and comes to live in us, but all the wonderful blessings He brings with Him must be worked out, in, and through our soul (mind, will, and emotions) so people can see them in the way we live our daily life. The goal is for people to see Jesus shining through us and want to receive Him also. People are looking for love, and this is why being selfish is so dangerous to the growth of God's kingdom. If we are selfish, we won't walk in love. We won't think of others because we are too wrapped up in thoughts, worries, and concerns about ourselves. We ask, "What will happen to me?" "What will I get?" "What about me?" "Who will do anything for me?" We think thoughts such as, "I want to be first" and "I need to look out for myself."

As Philippians 2:12–13 states, we should work with the Holy

Spirit enthusiastically to work out and complete our salvation with "reverence and awe and trembling." This means we should have a tender conscience before God, be watchful against temptation, and shrink from anything and everything that might offend God or discredit the name of Jesus.

It has occurred to me that often we may not even recognize when we are being selfish, simply because selfishness has been such a big part of our life. When we are still in diapers, we cry when we don't get our way, and we don't stop being upset when we don't get our way unless we work with God to overcome selfishness. We need to pray that God will reveal to us what we are doing anytime we are being selfish. I know that I don't want to be selfish, but I'm not sure I always recognize it. Self-preservation is a strong trait in all of us, and letting go of making sure we are taken care of and trusting ourselves to God cannot be done without much prayer and sensitivity to the Holy Spirit.

The Salvation of the Soul

Our will must be surrendered and submitted to God, which means we give up trying to control our circumstances and the people around us. There are, of course, some things in life we need to control, but most of them involve self-control. If the Holy Spirit is in control, then we will be full of life. But if we are in control, then although we are saved, we are still carnal (fleshly). Paul writes:

> The righteous and just requirement of the Law might be fully met in us who live and move not in the ways of the flesh but in the ways of the Spirit [our lives governed not by the standards and according to the dictates of the flesh, but controlled by the Holy Spirit].
>
> Romans 8:4

Let me ask you: What areas of your life have you submitted to the Holy Spirit?

- The use of your time, even your leisure time
- The entertainment you approve of and participate in
- The ways you spend your money
- Your thoughts—are they Spirit-controlled?
- Your mouth and the words you speak
- Your attitudes
- What you read and watch
- How you treat other people

You may ask, "How can I know what the Holy Spirit's guidance is in these areas?" Either God's Word will address the area you are dealing with or, if you are doing something that is not pleasing to God, you will feel a sense of discomfort inside of you. You lose your peace. This is the Holy Spirit convicting you of sin and trying to convince you to make a change.

We live life at such a fast pace and make quick decisions based on what we want, what we think, and how we feel that we usually don't even notice the discomfort. We simply go on doing things our way until we become miserable enough to start listening to the Lord.

Before pilots take planes into the air, they have a checklist they go through carefully to make sure everything is working as it should. Perhaps we should also have a checklist (at least a mental one) we go over a few times a day. It could include questions such as:

- Am I in too big of a hurry to hear God if He speaks?
- Am I doing what God desires and behaving in ways that please Him?

- Am I doing anything that bothers my conscience?
- Am I at peace with the choices I am making today?

When you pray, don't just talk to God; also take time to listen to Him. I recall once when I was praying, God spoke to my heart saying, "Joyce, it is time for your mouth to be saved." I was saved, but my salvation had not affected my mouth. I still gossiped, complained, criticized, spoke negatively often, was disrespectful to my husband at times, yelled at my children when I was frustrated with myself, and used my words in other negative ways. We can sincerely say that we want what God wants, but in order for self-will to be crucified, we have to do what is right and let it hurt while the flesh is dying.

Doing what is right even though it hurts means you are growing spiritually. So, you can be joyful, knowing that the pain means you are improving.

> *Doing what is right even though it hurts means you are growing spiritually.*

Galatians 5:16 says, "Walk and live [habitually] in the [Holy] Spirit [responsive to and controlled and guided by the Spirit]; then you will certainly not gratify the cravings and desires of the flesh (of human nature without God)."

Because the flesh and the spirit are continually opposed to each other, and because self-will is strong, overcoming the desires of our human nature and living habitually in the Spirit can be difficult. But don't give up, and no matter how many times you fall, get up and go again.

God's Toolbox

What kinds of things does God use to help us die to selfishness and mature spiritually? I call them tools in God's toolbox. A person who is in the process of dying to self may still want control in certain ways, so God uses circumstances beyond their control to eventually draw that person under His loving hand. I was very controlling when Dave and I were first married. But after I got serious in my relationship with God, I knew control was an attitude He wanted me to let go of and that I needed His help to do it. I found that God put me in situations I could not control and around people I could not control. This was one of the tools that helped me eventually die to self and become more pliable and moldable in His hand. Similar to what Paul mentions in Philippians 3:13–14, I have not arrived at the place of doing it perfectly, but I press toward the goal of letting go of control.

God also uses people who tell us to do things we don't want to do. And they are usually people who are important in our lives, such as an employer who could fire us from a job we want to keep, or a friend we don't want to lose. God may use people with personalities that irritate us, or someone who reminds us of a person we dislike.

I did not like people who reminded me of my father, but for a season in my life, God seemed to surround me with them. I had to learn how to deal with them in godly ways. God wants us to mature to the point where circumstances beyond our control don't get us out of control, but instead we trust Him. He gives us self-control for the purpose the phrase indicates: so we can control ourselves.

When I first read that wives should submit and adapt themselves to their husbands (Ephesians 5:22), I was far from obedient in this area. But as I fell more deeply in love with Jesus and wanted to be obedient to Him, I noticed that Dave would occasionally tell me to do or not to do something I didn't agree with. I knew that God had His toolbox out again and was working on me. I didn't always pass my test, and when I didn't, I got to take it over at a later time. In God's school we never fail; we just get to keep taking the test until we pass it.

God's Word tells us to obey the authority over us, including civil authority (Romans 13:1). It also instructs us to be submissive to one another (Ephesians 5:21) and to submit to God (James 4:7). We encounter some kind of authority almost everywhere we go. It does not exist in order for one person to rule over another, but so we can have order rather than chaos. The person in authority may not always be right in their decisions, but we should pray for them and let God reveal that to them instead of trying to correct them ourselves.

Circumstances beyond Our Control

God allows circumstances that are out of our control to eventually teach us to stay calm during adversity (Psalm 94:13), and He actually uses them to harden us to difficulties, according to Isaiah 41:10:

> Fear not [there is nothing to fear], for I am with you; do not look around you in terror and be dismayed, for I am your God. I will strengthen and harden you to difficulties, yes, I will help you; yes, I will hold you up and retain you with My [victorious] right hand of rightness and justice.

Certain situations that once upset me don't bother me at all now because I have been through them again and again. God has hardened me to difficulties. I have died to self in this area.

We should never be surprised when we go through hard times or when things don't work out as we would like. First Peter 4:12 says, "Beloved, do not be amazed and bewildered at the fiery ordeal which is taking place to test your quality, as though something strange (unusual and alien to you and your position) were befalling you."

God wants us to be submissive to Him, but unmanageable to the devil. James 1:2–3 tells us that trials of all kinds bring out the fruit of patience. In fact, I have told people in my life that they brought a lot of things out of me before we got around to patience.

> God wants us to be submissive to Him, but unmanageable to the devil.

We are to consider the trials we face "wholly joyful," knowing that they will bring out patience (James 1:2). When patience has done its work in us, we will be "perfectly and fully developed [with no defects], lacking in nothing" (James 1:4). When we are patient, the devil cannot use our emotions against us. Developing this kind of patience requires learning to trust God, knowing that He is good, and believing that He will never allow us to be tempted more than we can bear (1 Corinthians 10:13).

Divine Disappointments

God may sometimes arrange for divine disappointments to get us to the point where we trust Him and don't get depressed and discouraged when we don't get what we want or expect. Or He may even allow us to experience a divine failure, so we don't think more highly of ourselves than we should (Romans 12:3).

The apostle Peter is a good example of this. Jesus told the disciples that all of them would fall away (Matthew 26:31). Peter said he would never do that, even if he had to die first (Matthew 26:35). Yet, Peter did deny Jesus not once but three times (Matthew 26:69–75). This worked in him a humility he desperately needed in order to fulfill God's call on his life.

Going through trials is painful, but they bring healing and strength. It is better to submit to them rather than to resist them. Let God do the work He wants to do in you so you can be the person He wants you to be.

At times, the trials in our life are the result of the devil's attack against us, and we should resist him. At other times, the difficulties we face are arranged by God for our good. How can we know the difference? Things from the devil are evil in nature because he is a liar (John 8:44), and he only comes "to steal and kill and destroy" (John 10:10). In contrast, things that are divinely directed may be uncomfortable, but they are not destructive. They don't steal from us or destroy us, but they ultimately make us better. Even things that the devil brings against us to harm us can ultimately work out for our good if we trust God (Romans 8:28).

CHAPTER 21

The Living Dead

*Whereas she who lives in pleasure and self-gratification
[giving herself up to luxury and self-indulgence] is dead
even while she [still] lives.*

1 Timothy 5:6

According to 1 Timothy 5:6, selfish people who live to make themselves happy are dead even though they are alive. I think this means they are dead inside. God told Adam that if he did what He had told him not to do, he would die (Genesis 2:17). Adam and Eve did disobey God, and though they didn't die physically at that time, everything changed for them. They experienced fear for the first time, they felt a need to hide from God (Genesis 3:10), and although the Bible doesn't say this exactly, I think they lost their joy and peace. The life and light they had inside of them went out when they sinned and did not repent.

When we learn how to truly love people, we pass from death to life, according to 1 John 3:14: "We know that we have passed from death to life, because we love each other. Anyone who does not love remains in death" (NIV). When we love others, we have joy, power, and peace—and we are filled with life.

This verse refers to spiritual life or death, not physical life or death. The world is full of what we will call "the walking dead." You can see it on their faces and in their attitudes. You can hear it in their words, and you can recognize it in the way they treat other people. They are unhappy, and unhappy people tend to make others unhappy, too.

My father was extremely selfish. He didn't care who he hurt as long as he got what he wanted. He was also very unhappy and seemed to delight in making others unhappy, too. He was actually annoyed when anyone around him was joyous and happy. Sadly, the world we live in today is filled with people who are like he was. They are unhappy because they live for themselves and do not care who they hurt as long as they get what they want. I am grateful that we can choose to live an unselfish life that leads to joy and actually gives us power over the devil. Always remember that we overcome evil with good (Romans 12:21).

Dead Man Walking

Selfish people are often lonely people, but they don't realize that being selfish can lead to loneliness. I mentioned in the introduction that I believe selfishness is like living in solitary confinement in a prison, because there is no one in your life other than yourself. Most prison cells are approximately six feet by nine feet. Just imagine being in a space like that by yourself, perhaps for many years. That in itself would be torture.

When someone is on death row, they are in solitary confinement, living each day just waiting to die. They are referred to as "dead men walking." Surely this is not what we want to be.

As believers in Christ, we have His power in us, and, very importantly, we have His love in us. We have what the world wants and needs, and all we have to do is get ourselves off our minds and learn to give love away.

As Jesus says in Mark 8:34, "If anyone intends to come after Me, let him deny himself [forget, ignore, disown, and lose sight of himself and his own interests] and take up his cross, and [joining Me as a disciple and siding with My party] follow with Me [continually, cleaving steadfastly to Me]." I hope that by now this doesn't sound as frightening as it may have seemed in the beginning of the book. Anytime we do things God's way, our lives improve and we experience His joy and peace.

Three Ways to Express Love to People

There are many ways to show people we love them, and even though I have written a chapter on it in this book, I would like to devote this section of this chapter to three specific ways we can all express love to others: be merciful, be quick to forgive, and resist the temptation to judge.

1. Be merciful.

> So be merciful (sympathetic, tender, responsive, and compassionate) even as your Father is [all these].
>
> Luke 6:36

If we remember that we need mercy ourselves, it is easier to show mercy to other people. I describe showing mercy as withholding punishment that is due and giving forgiveness instead. Mercy is comforting, soothing, and healing. It is beautiful, and God's mercies are new every morning (Lamentations 3:22–23 ESV), so perhaps ours should be too. As God's children, we should never have an attitude of revenge or spend our time and energy trying to retaliate against someone who has hurt us. We have the privilege of giving mercy because God has given mercy to us. Have you received God's mercy, or are you still punishing yourself for mistakes you have made, even though Jesus has already taken your punishment and forgiven you? If we don't receive mercy, we cannot give it to others.

If you don't receive mercy, you cannot give it to others.

Jesus is full of mercy toward us. He became our "merciful (sympathetic) and faithful High Priest in the things related to God, to make atonement and propitiation for the people's sins" (Hebrews 2:17). Simply reading this scripture and realizing the great mercy Jesus has for me makes me relax and feel more comfortable. Just imagine how much better our relationships with people would be if we offered them mercy instead of anger when they make mistakes. Being angry is harder on us than on the person we are angry with. There are, of course, times when we need to correct people in an effort to help them learn to do things God's way, but we should focus on being merciful and pray for people to follow God in all their ways.

Growing up, I never received mercy from my father. Every mistake brought punishment of some kind, and I lived in fear of him. We could eliminate so much fear in the world if people could count on one another for mercy instead of punishment. As I said, sometimes people do need to experience consequences, but that doesn't mean we can't also give them mercy in our attitude toward them. Even when God does chastise us, He says it is because He loves us (Hebrews 12:6; Revelation 3:19).

God is abundant in mercy. The Bible mentions His mercy and compassion hundreds of times. The fact that He is merciful does not remove our responsibility to do the best we can, but it does give us an opportunity to repent and make a change for the better. God's mercy toward us brings us joy, and our mercy toward others will give them and us joy.

Consider this small sample of what God's Word says about His mercy:

> The Lord is gracious and full of compassion, slow to anger and abounding in mercy and loving-kindness. The Lord is good to all, and His tender mercies are over all His works [the entirety of things created].
>
> Psalm 145:8–9

> To Him Who [earnestly] remembered us in our low estate and imprinted us [on His heart], for His mercy and loving-kindness endure forever; and rescued us from our enemies, for His mercy and loving-kindness endure forever.
>
> Psalm 136:23–24

If we want to be like God, we need to study mercy and be ready to extend it to others generously. We should also receive it for ourselves when we need it, which may be daily or even several times each day. The more we learn to receive God's mercy and realize how amazingly wonderful it is, the easier it will be for us to give it away to others.

Paul writes in Colossians that we are to "put on tender mercies" (Colossians 3:12 NKJV). This means mercy is something we decide to give to others, not something we wait to feel like giving. In John 8:1–11, we read the story of a woman who was caught in adultery. The Pharisees (religious leaders) put her in front of a crowd to stone her, because stoning was the punishment for her behavior according to their law. Jesus was present when this took place, and the Pharisees hoped to trap Him into saying something they could use against Him by asking Him what should be done with her. Instead of recommending punishment, Jesus said, "Let him who is without sin among you be the first to throw a stone at her" (v. 7), and one by one, they all walked away.

Notice that it was the religious law keepers who were quick to embarrass the woman in front of the crowd and to want her stoned to death. Legalistic self-righteous people are often quick to judge, criticize, and punish. But true followers of Jesus who have received mercy want to give mercy also. Which one of us is so perfect that we never need mercy? Certainly not I. How about you? We are to do unto others as we want them to do to us (Matthew 7:12). This is referred to as the Golden Rule in Christianity. Just imagine what a different world we would live in if everyone followed this one principle. Is there someone in your life right now who needs you to show mercy to them?

Is there someone in your life right now who needs you to show mercy to them?

2. Be quick to forgive.

> As the Lord has forgiven you, so you also must forgive.
>
> Colossians 3:13 ESV

If we would give away the same kind of forgiveness we receive from God, our lives would be much happier. When we hold unforgiveness against someone, we may think we are punishing them, but actually we are imprisoning ourselves in hatred and bitterness. Refusing to forgive is like taking poison yourself and hoping your enemy will die.

Forgiveness is a decision about how we will treat people; it isn't a feeling. I may not like a person, but I can still love them and forgive them if they hurt me.

Often, people don't forgive because they think it is too hard. But forgiving is a lot easier than living filled with hatred. When you forgive an offender, you are released from further torment, and you release the person who hurt you into God's hands, knowing that He will deal with them properly. God is a God of justice, and He always makes wrong things right.

Ask yourself daily if you are angry with anyone. If so, ask God to help you let go of the offense and trust Him to deal with it properly.

Hatred is ugly, but forgiveness is beautiful.

Hatred is ugly, but forgiveness is beautiful.

3. Resist the temptation to judge.

> "Judge not, that you be not judged."
>
> Matthew 7:1 ESV

We will be judged in the same way in which we judge others. Have you ever been adversely judged by anyone? I have, and it hurts when people think or say things about us that are not true. Often, when people judge others, they don't even know what they are talking about. They may be merely passing on gossip they heard, or perhaps they judged at a glance, which God's Word tells us not to do (John 7:24). If you don't like the way you look and are insecure about it, and you are introduced to someone who has flawless skin and is slim and attractive, you may decide at a glance that you don't like them, but the root of the dislike is jealousy. If you take the time to truly get to know them, you might find a really good friend.

I recently read something about myself on the internet, and it was news to me. It said that I buy all my clothes at a store that is very expensive. All I could say is, "If I do, where are all those nice clothes? They're not in my closet." The person who posted that wrong information simply wanted to portray me as someone who spends huge sums of money on my clothing, thinking that would cause others to judge me also. This is the behavior of someone who is inherently mean-spirited and probably jealous. Be careful about believing everything you read or hear about another person and passing judgment on them based on that information.

If a person does buy all of their clothing from an expensive store, that is between the individual and God. It is certainly none of my business, nor anyone else's. Social media is known as a place where uninformed people gossip and spread their lies and rumors to thousands of other people. Don't be foolish and believe a bad report about someone unless it is confirmed in the mouth of two or three witnesses (Deuteronomy 17:6; 2 Corinthians 13:1 NKJV). The witnesses should be reliable (Proverbs 14:5).

We should protect one another and cover each other with love and not be eager to jump to conclusions that we don't know to be true. Love always believes the best of every person (1 Corinthians 13:7).

There are many other ways to show love, but these three give you an idea of how love behaves.

Developing Loving Attitudes

I had to *develop* a merciful, forgiving, nonjudgmental attitude because, for many years, I didn't have one. Being merciful, forgiving, and nonjudgmental didn't come naturally to me. If you are not merciful but tend to be more rigid and legalistic, I urge you to pray that God will help you develop a merciful attitude toward others. The merciful are blessed for they shall receive mercy (Matthew 5:7). Do the same if you feel your attitude is unforgiving or judgmental.

James writes that "mercy triumphs over judgment" (James 2:13 NIV). In other words, people who give mercy are greater than those who judge. No one really has a right to judge another person. We can and should judge sin, but we cannot judge people, because we don't know what they have been through or what they know or don't know. The judging of people is up to God, not to us (James 4:12). We have civil law and judges who judge those who break the law, but I am talking about something different here. God gives us mercy we don't deserve, and we should be ready to extend that mercy to others if they hurt or offend us. We may think they don't deserve mercy, but that's the beauty of mercy. It is a gift and cannot be earned or deserved. As I mentioned previously, there may be consequences for doing wrong, but our attitude toward people should be merciful.

> As God gives you mercy you don't deserve, give mercy to those who have hurt you.

God is so rich in mercy that even while we were still dead in sin, He made us alive together in fellowship and in union with Christ. It is because of His mercy and love that we are saved, not because of anything we have or haven't done (Ephesians 2:4–5).

People who are unwilling to give mercy to others are selfish. They would rather keep their anger and critical attitudes than give mercy, but these same people will want mercy when they have done something wrong. Selfish people want what they are not willing to give to others.

God's ways bring life and love. If we do not operate in His ways, we are full of death and misery. This is a terrible condition to be in, but one that is easy to fix. All we need to do is admit our sin, ask for forgiveness, receive it, and be ready to let the Holy Spirit help us develop loving, merciful, and forgiving attitudes toward people. Don't feed selfishness by giving in to it. Resist it just as you would resist any other sin. Remember, as Christians, we know we have passed from death to life by the fact that we love each other (1 John 3:14).

CHAPTER 22

Complete Surrender

I appeal to you therefore, brethren, and beg of you in view of [all] the mercies of God, to make a decisive dedication of your bodies [presenting all your members and faculties] as a living sacrifice, holy (devoted, consecrated) and well pleasing to God, which is your reasonable (rational, intelligent) service and spiritual worship.

Romans 12:1

Romans 12:1 teaches us that it is our reasonable service and worship to God to present everything we are to God and to dedicate all of our members and faculties, which means basically everything about us, to God for His use. This would include our mind, mouth, emotions, will, time, energy, finances, hands, feet, heart—every aspect of who we are. With this in mind, are you ready for a complete surrender?

When we receive Jesus as our Lord and Savior, we experience salvation, but we may not completely surrender everything about us in the moment of salvation. We may want to, but as we walk with God, we may realize that we want to hold on to certain things in our lives because we have not yet understood how trustworthy God is. Complete surrender is both a decision and a journey.

Our commitment to the Lord must be a sincere one. When I ask you if you are ready to make a complete surrender, I urge you to think about it seriously before answering. This is a big commitment, but one that will eventually bring you contentment, peace, and joy you have never known. It will also open the windows of heaven, and unimaginable blessings will be poured out on you.

People are afraid to stop being selfish because they think that if they don't take care of themselves or if they give themselves to blessing others instead of seeking blessings for themselves, they will never get what they want. But the opposite is true. When we truly, completely surrender to the Lord, He will, at the right time, give us the desires of our heart (Psalm 37:4).

Change

It should be understood that when we make a complete surrender to God there will be changes in our life. We may not like all of them initially. We often want our circumstances to change, but *we* don't want to change. But our circumstances won't change until we do. I have discovered in my life that many of my circumstances have remained

> Your circumstances won't change until you do.

the same, but I have changed so much that they don't bother me now. I actually see how foolish it was to be upset and frustrated by some of the silly things that once bothered me. The more we die to self, the less we will be upset by inconveniences or by people who don't do what we want them to do.

When we change, we are transformed. *Transform* implies a major change in form, nature, or function. It means to "change in character or condition: convert."[29] God does the work of transformation in our spirit when we accept Christ as our Savior, but the same work must be done in our soul, and that's what dying to self is all about. In case you have forgotten, dying to self is no longer living according to what we think, want, and feel. Instead, it is living according to God's will no matter how we feel about it. We want to be in agreement with God at all times. When we are born again, we get a new nature in our spirit, but the old nature still clings to us, and we need to learn not to let our old nature rule us anymore. Romans 6:11 tells us we are to consider ourselves dead to sin. I realized one day that God's Word doesn't say that sin dies; it says we are dead to sin. Sin will always be around, tempting us to do the wrong thing, but we can learn to do the right thing even though the devil is pressuring us to sin. The real us, the born-again us with the new nature God has given us, does not want to sin. It is our flesh that is weak.

God's desire is to not only transform us but also to restore us.

He wants us, His children, to be brought back to the original state He intended for us from the beginning of time. He has already paid the price to give back to us everything the devil has stolen from us over the years. Perhaps he has stolen your confidence, your security, your ability to trust God and people, or your faith. Maybe he is holding you captive through fear and doubt. God can reverse all of that if we will believe we are redeemed. Colossians 1:13–14 says, "For he has rescued us from the dominion of darkness and brought us into the kingdom of the Son he loves, in whom we have redemption, the forgiveness of sins" (NIV).

All we need to do is surrender our will to His. We must understand that we cannot have God's will and our will simultaneously, at least not most of the time. Sometimes they are in agreement, but often they are not. Eventually our will and His will become the same, but initially they are usually very far apart, and a deep work of transformation must take place in our souls for them to become one. We will get there little by little as we work with the Holy Spirit while His grace changes us.

God doesn't want us to be *under* something all the time—under attack, under pressure, under stress, or under anything except His authority. He wants us to know and use the authority and power that belong to us in and through Him. This scripture helps us remember that we have power over the works of the devil:

Behold! I have given you authority and power to trample upon serpents and scorpions, and [physical and mental strength and ability] over all the power that the enemy [possesses]; and nothing shall in any way harm you.

Luke 10:19

Everything changes except God. He is the same yesterday, today, and forever (Hebrews 13:8). Change is a sign that we are growing, a sign that we are alive. It is a fact of life. It can be initially frightening, but eventually refreshing.

In Deuteronomy 8 God tells the Israelites to obey all His commands that they might "live and multiply and go in and possess the land" He had promised them (v. 1). They were already alive, so what does it mean when He says that they may live? He means *really* live—to live a life that is amazing, one you are excited to greet each day when you wake up. He told the Israelites He would test them to see if they would keep His commandments or not (v. 2). It is easy to love God and keep His commands when everything is going our way, but what about when it isn't? Will you still obey God even when you do not get an instant reward and have no idea if you will ever get one or not? Will you obey God when your circumstances are difficult and nothing in your life seems fair?

God told the Israelites that He allowed them to go through difficult tests in order to take them into a good land, one that flowed with every good thing they could imagine (vv. 1–9). Then in verses 10–20, He tells them not to forget Him when they have come into the good land and have all they want, or they will perish.

It is very important to the Lord that we love Him as devotedly in hard times as we do in good times.

Metamorphosis

The amplification of 2 Corinthians 3:18 teaches us that as we continue looking into God's Word, we will be transfigured into His image. Other translations say we will be transformed into His image (NIV, NKJV, ESV). The Greek word for *changed* or *transformed* is the same root word used for *metamorphosis*, which means to undergo a complete change.[30] Not only is this kind of change hard, but it can also be confusing. When we are changing, we are

> *When you are changing, you are no longer what you once were but not yet what you will be.*

no longer what we once were, but we are not yet what we will be. We feel disoriented and confused. If you feel this way, don't give up, because clarity will come.

Think of a caterpillar becoming a butterfly. No two creatures could be more different from each other. Butterflies are very beautiful, but caterpillars are known to be pests, and they devour food plants. When the process of change begins, caterpillars molt (shed their skin). This occurs several times. Similarly, as believers we must shed many things during our transformation process. We may shed wrong thinking, bad attitudes, unforgiveness, disobedience, stubbornness, rebellion, jealousy, and pride, among others. The list is endless.

Once the molting is complete, the caterpillar spins a button of silk that adheres to a twig, leaf, branch, or other support. In our similar stage, we cling to Jesus. We learn to abide (remain) in Him (John 15:1–8). As the caterpillar clings to the support, all of its skin peels off and a hard chrysalis is revealed.

Just as caterpillars become butterflies in the secrecy of the chrysalis, the metamorphosis you and I undergo is a process that takes place in private. I believe that what God does in us is between Him and us and should be kept private for the most part. At times, we wouldn't know how to explain what we feel anyway. We simply know things are changing, but we are not sure what is changing or how it's changing.

The amount of time spent in the chrysalis varies depending on the kind of butterfly. It may be days, weeks, or months. But while in the chrysalis, everything in the caterpillar turns to liquid. From that state, it is formed into the beautiful butterfly it is destined to become. We should become the same way in the Lord's hands—pliable and easily reshaped for a new purpose.

Tadpoles become frogs through metamorphosis. Moths, bees, wasps, ants, and beetles (including ladybugs) grow through a unique life cycle called complete metamorphosis, which has four distinct stages: egg, larva, pupa, and adult.

Just as different insects go through various stages according to a variety of time frames, we cannot expect our change to be exactly like someone else's, because we are all different, and God's will and purpose for each of us is different. We should not compare our rate of change to anyone else's. God knows what is right for each of us, and our job is to trust Him completely, knowing that He loves us and is working His perfect plan for our future. No matter how big my problem is when I am fighting it, I have pain, but when I totally trust God to take care of it, the pain ceases and peace comes.

During metamorphosis, the pupa at times does not even appear to be alive. We may feel that way sometimes as God is changing us. Or at least we wonder if we will live through all the changes taking place in our lives.

When the time is right for the transformed caterpillar to emerge from its chrysalis, it breaks out by means of thrashing movements and is now a butterfly. At first, it is weak, soft, and limp, but as it exercises its wings, it gradually gains strength to begin its new life. Similarly, as we continue to allow God to transform us, we gain more strength and become more like Him every day.

Changed into the Image of Christ

Jesus is morally excellent, and by the time we go through transformation, we are on our way to becoming the same way. We begin to do what is godly, make godly choices, speak in godly ways, have godly attitudes, treat people well, and use our money and other resources wisely.

God told Adam to "be fruitful, multiply, and fill the earth, and subdue it [using all its vast resources in the service of God and man]" (Genesis 1:28). This scripture teaches us that God never intended us to use what we have or what He has provided in a selfish and self-centered way, but to serve Him and help others.

God made human beings in His own image and likeness (Genesis 1:26–27). The devil, through deception, introduced sin, but God has destined us to be changed back to His original intention. Whatever we are destined for, we can never be completely satisfied without.

I hope that by now you understand more of what I mean when I say we must die to live. Let our goal be to say with the apostle Paul, "It is no longer I who live, but Christ lives in me" (Galatians 2:20 NKJV) and "God forbid that I should boast except in the cross of our Lord Jesus Christ, by whom the world has been crucified to me, and I to the world" (Galatians 6:14 NKJV). And let us say with the apostle John, "He must increase, but I must decrease" (John 3:30).

We are free to enjoy what is good and what God has created, but we must remember that we are lights in the world (Philippians 2:15 NKJV), and light has no fellowship with darkness (2 Corinthians 6:14).

A friend asked me recently how to manage emotions. He said, "When I get angry at my wife, I eventually talk to her, but it takes me several days to do it. How do you do it right away?" I told him that my relationship with the Lord is more important to me than feeding my anger, and that I have learned over a period of time that I don't have to feel like doing the right thing to do it. If you can remember these two truths from this book—that your relationship with

You don't have to feel like doing the right thing to do it.

God is more important than your emotions and that you can do what is right when you don't feel like it—I believe they will help you when you are faced with making a difficult decision.

The Teacup Story

Let me end this book with a story I have shared many times. There are various versions of it, but they all make the same point. Even if you have heard it previously, it is the perfect ending for this book:

> There was a couple who used to go to England to shop in beautiful stores. They both liked antiques and pottery and especially teacups. One day, on their twenty-fifth wedding anniversary, in a beautiful shop they saw a beautiful teacup.
>
> They said, "May we see that? We've never seen one quite so beautiful."
>
> As the lady handed it to them, suddenly the teacup spoke. "You don't understand," it said. "I haven't always been like this. There was a time when I was red and I was clay. My master took me and rolled me and patted me over and over and I yelled out, 'Let me alone,' but he only smiled and said, 'Not yet.'
>
> "Then I was placed on a spinning wheel," the teacup said, "and suddenly I was spun around and around and around. 'Stop it! I'm getting dizzy!' I screamed. But the master only nodded and said, 'Not yet.'
>
> "Then he put me in the oven. I never felt such heat. I wondered why he wanted to burn me, and I yelled and knocked at the door. I could see him through the

opening, and I could read his lips as he shook his head. 'Not yet.'

"Finally the door opened, he put me on the shelf, and I began to cool. 'There, that's better,' I said. And he brushed and painted me all over. The fumes were horrible. I thought I would gag. 'Stop it, stop it!' I cried. He only nodded. 'Not yet.'

"Then suddenly he put me back into the oven, not like the first one. This was twice as hot, and I knew I would suffocate. I begged. I pleaded. I screamed. I cried. All the time I could see him through the opening nodding his head, saying, 'Not yet.'

"Then I knew there wasn't any hope. I would never make it. I was ready to give up. But the door opened, and he took me out and placed me on the shelf. One hour later he handed me a mirror, and I couldn't believe it was me. 'It's beautiful. I'm beautiful.' "

" 'I want you to remember, then,' he said. 'I know it hurts to be rolled and patted, but if I had left you alone, you would have dried up. I know it made you dizzy to spin around on the wheel, but if I had stopped, you would have crumbled. I knew it hurt and was hot and disagreeable in the oven, but if I hadn't put you there, you would have cracked. I know the fumes were bad when I brushed and painted you all over, but if I hadn't done that, you never would have hardened; you would not have had any color in your life. And if I hadn't put you back in that second oven, you wouldn't survive for very long because the hardness would not have held. Now you are a finished product. You are what I had in mind when I first began with you.' " (Author unknown)

The process of maturing in Christ and being transformed into His image is difficult, and while we are going through it, we usually don't understand what is happening to us. But, if you don't give up, you, like the beautiful teacup, will be completely changed and admired for your spiritual beauty in Christ.

CONCLUSION

I think this may be one of the most important books I have written. I've wanted to write it for a long time, but wasn't sure how people would respond to a book about dying to self and living unselfishly. I am being obedient to God in writing it, and now the rest is up to Him.

I pray you have enjoyed this book and learned a lot from it. I also pray that it has given you understanding regarding the maturing process we must go through to become who and what God wants us to be. The teacup story is a great example of this. People often look at a finished product and have no understanding of what it took to complete it. If you have ever contracted someone to build you a new home, you can use that as an example, too. What is now your lovely home was once a big hole in the ground!

It is my fervent desire that you have seen the disadvantages of being selfish and that you are ready to try living God's way, which prioritizes love, sacrifice, giving, serving, and helping other people be happy. I can promise you that, if you try God's way, though it may take a while for your flesh to adjust, you will eventually be free from the prison of self.

God loves you more than you could ever imagine, and His desire is for you to enjoy the best life possible. Norman MacEwan said, "We make a living by what we get, but we make a life by what we give."[31] I can say without hesitation that this statement is true. My walk with God has been long and often difficult, but at the same time glorious and truly life-changing. I pray you will make a complete surrender to Him and His way today. I encourage you to buy at least one more book and give it to someone as a gift. If enough of us become unselfish followers of Jesus, we can change the world.

Do you have a real relationship with Jesus?

God loves you! He created you to be a special, unique, one-of-a-kind individual, and He has a specific purpose and plan for your life. And through a personal relationship with your Creator—God—you can discover a way of life that will truly satisfy your soul.

No matter who you are, what you've done, or where you are in your life right now, God's love and grace are greater than your sin—your mistakes. Jesus willingly gave His life so you can receive forgiveness from God and have new life in Him. He's just waiting for you to invite Him to be your Savior and Lord.

If you are ready to commit your life to Jesus and follow Him, all you have to do is ask Him to forgive your sins and give you a fresh start in the life you are meant to live. Begin by praying this prayer...

> *Lord Jesus, thank You for giving Your life for me and forgiving me of my sins so I can have a personal relationship with You. I am sincerely sorry for the mistakes I've made, and I know I need You to help me live right.*
>
> *Your Word says in Romans 10:9, "If you declare with your mouth, 'Jesus is Lord,' and believe in your heart that God raised him from the dead, you will be saved" (NIV). I believe You are the Son of God and confess You as my Savior and Lord. Take me just as I am, and work in my heart, making me the person You want me to be. I want to live for You, Jesus, and I am so grateful that You are giving me a fresh start in my new life with You today.*
>
> *I love You, Jesus!*

It's so amazing to know that God loves us so much! He wants to have a deep, intimate relationship with us that grows every day as we spend time with Him in prayer and Bible study. And we want to encourage you in your new life in Christ.

Please visit joycemeyer.org/KnowJesus to request Joyce's book *A New Way of Living*, which is our gift to you. We also have other free resources online to help you make progress in pursuing everything God has for you.

Congratulations on your fresh start in your life in Christ! We hope to hear from you soon.

NOTES

1. John F. MacArthur, *Hard to Believe: The High Cost and Infinite Value of Following Jesus* (Thomas Nelson Inc., 2006), 2.
2. Watchman Nee, *Spiritual Authority* (Christian Fellowship, 1972), 69.

3. BrainyQuote, https://www.brainyquote.com/quotes/joseph_joubert _105575.

4. Mahatma Gandhi, *Ethical Religion* (S. Ganesan, 1922), 62.

5. Joseph Hartropp, "Amazing Grace: 7 Quotes from the Slaver-Turned-Preacher John Newton," *Christian Today*, July 24, 2017, https://www .christiantoday.com/article/amazing-grace-7-quotes-from-the-slaver -turned-preacher-john-newton/111066.htm.

6. Derek Prince, *By Grace Alone: Finding Freedom and Purging Legalism from Your Life* (Baker Publishing Group, 2013).

7. A. B. Simpson, *Walking in the Spirit* (Christian Alliance Publishing, 1889), chap. 16.

8. "Prompt," *The American Heritage Dictionary of the English Language*, 5th ed. (HarperCollins, 2022).

9. Charles Haddon Spurgeon, *Evening by Evening: Or, Readings at Eventide for the Family or the Closet* (Passmore and Alabaster, 1868), 335.

10. Steve Maraboli, "Selfish People...," Tumblr.com, May 16, 2015, https://stevemaraboli.tumblr.com/post/119131243730/selfish-people -tend-to-only-be-good-to-themselves.

11. Sija Mafu, "7 Sobering Stephen Kendrick Quotes about Unconditional Love," Motivated2Inspire, September 6, 2021, https:// motivated2inspire.com/37-stephen-kendrick-quotes-that-express -his-love-for-god.

12. "Die to Self and Live Wholly to Him," Prince of Preachers, June 15, 2017, https://www.princeofpreachers.org/quotes/die-to-self-and -live-wholly-to-him.

13. Mark Batterson, *Going All In: One Decision Can Change Everything* (Zondervan, 2013), 11.

14. Roger Steer, *George Müller: Delighted in God* (Crown, 2000).

15. "μακροθυμία," Blue Letter Bible, https://www.blueletterbible.org /lexicon/g3115/mgnt/tr/0-1.

16. BrainyQuote, https://www.brainyquote.com/quotes/ann_landers _104934.

17. "Diakonos," Bible Hub, https://biblehub.com/greek/1249.htm.

18. Anne Frank, "Give," in *The Works of Anne Frank* (Greenwood Press, 1959).

19. Simone Weil, Letter to Joë Bousquet, April 13, 1942, in Simone Pétrement, *Simone Weil: A Life*, translated by Raymond Rosenthal (Pantheon, 1976).

20. QuoteFancy, https://quotefancy.com/quote/758140/John-Bunyan-You -have-not-lived-today-until-you-have-done-something-for -someone-who-can.

21. "Practicing Gratitude for Better Health and Well-Being," University of Utah Health, November 19, 2021, https://healthcare .utah.edu/healthfeed/2021/11/practicing-gratitude-better-health -and-well-being; Linda Wasmer Andrews, "How Gratitude Helps You Sleep at Night," *Psychology Today*, November 9, 2011, https:// www.psychologytoday.com/us/blog/minding-the-body/201111 /how-gratitude-helps-you-sleep-night.

22. "Anger: How It Affects People," Better Health Channel, n.d., https:// www.betterhealth.vic.gov.au/health/healthyliving/anger-how -it-affects-people.

23. "The End of Anxiety," GeorgeMuller.org, March 26, 2015, https:// www.georgemuller.org/quotes/the-end-of-anxiety.

24. "Trust," American Dictionary of the English Language (online), https://webstersdictionary1828.com/Dictionary/trust.

25. "Anapauó," Bible Hub, https://biblehub.com/greek/373.htm.

26. Ashleigh Brilliant, *I Try to Take It One Day at a Time, but Sometimes Several Days Attack Me at Once*, Brilliant Thoughts 6 (Brilliant Enterprises, 1987).

27. "Zóopoieó," Bible Hub, https://biblehub.com/greek/2227.htm.

28. "Quicken," Dictionary.com, https://www.dictionary.com/browse /quicken.

29. "Transform," *Merriam-Webster.com Dictionary*, https://www.merriam -webster.com/dictionary/transform.

30. "Metamorphoó,"Bible Hub, https://biblehub.com/greek/3339.htm.

31. Quoted in *The Forbes Scrapbook of Thoughts on the Business of Life* (B. C. Forbes & Sons, 1950).

ABOUT THE AUTHOR

Joyce Meyer is one of the world's leading practical Bible teachers and a *New York Times* bestselling author. Joyce's books have helped millions of people find hope and restoration through Jesus Christ. Joyce's program, *Enjoying Everyday Life*, is broadcast on television, radio, and online to millions worldwide in over 110 languages.

Through Joyce Meyer Ministries, Joyce teaches internationally on a number of topics with a particular focus on how the Word of God applies to our everyday lives. Her candid communication style allows her to share openly and practically about her experiences so others can apply what she has learned to their lives.

Joyce has authored more than 140 books, which have been translated into more than 160 languages, and over 39 million of her books have been distributed worldwide. Bestsellers include *Power Thoughts*; *The Confident Woman*; *Look Great, Feel Great*; *Starting Your Day Right*; *Ending Your Day Right*; *Approval Addiction*; *How to Hear from God*; *Beauty for Ashes*; and *Battlefield of the Mind*.

Joyce's passion to help people who are hurting is foundational to the vision of Hand of Hope, the missions arm of Joyce Meyer Ministries. Each year Hand of Hope provides millions of meals for the hungry and malnourished, installs freshwater wells in poor and remote areas, provides critical relief after natural disasters, and offers free medical and dental care to thousands through their hospitals and clinics worldwide. Through Project GRL, women and children are rescued from human trafficking and provided safe places to receive an education, nutritious meals, and the love of God.

JOYCE MEYER MINISTRIES

U.S. & FOREIGN OFFICE
ADDRESSES

Joyce Meyer Ministries
P.O. Box 655
Fenton, MO 63026
USA
(866) 480-1528

Joyce Meyer Ministries—Canada
P.O. Box 7700
Vancouver, BC V6B 4E2
Canada
(800) 868-1002

Joyce Meyer Ministries—Australia
Locked Bag 77
Mansfield Delivery Centre
Queensland 4122
Australia
+61 7 3349 1200

Joyce Meyer Ministries—England
P.O. Box 8267
Reading, RG6 9TX
United Kingdom
+44 1753 831102

Joyce Meyer Ministries—South Africa
Unit EB06, East Block, Tannery Park
23 Belmont Road
Rondebosch, Cape Town, South Africa, 7700
+27 21 701 1056

Joyce Meyer Ministries—Francophonie
29 avenue Maurice Chevalier
77330 Ozoir la Ferriere
France

Joyce Meyer Ministries—Germany
Postfach 761001
22060 Hamburg
Germany
+49 (0)40 / 88 88 4 11 11

Joyce Meyer Ministries—Netherlands
Postbus 55
7000 HB Doetinchem
The Netherlands
+31 (0)26 20 22 100

Joyce Meyer Ministries—Russia
P.O. Box 789
Moscow 101000
Russia
+7 (495) 727-14-68

OTHER BOOKS BY JOYCE MEYER

The Word, the Name, the Blood
Woman to Woman
You Can Begin Again
Your Battles Belong to the Lord*

JOYCE MEYER SPANISH TITLES

Amar a la gente que es muy difícil de amar (Loving People
Who Are Hard to Love)
Auténtica y única (Authentically, Uniquely You)
Belleza en lugar de cenizas (Beauty for Ashes)
Bendicion en el desorden (Blessed in the Mess)
Buena salud, buena vida (Good Health, Good Life)
Cambia tus palabras, cambia tu vida (Change Your Words, Change Your Life)
El campo de batalla de la mente (Battlefield of the Mind)
Cómo envejecer sin avejentarse (How to Age without Getting Old)
Como formar buenos habitos y romper malos habitos (Making Good Habits,
Breaking Bad Habits)
La conexión de la mente (The Mind Connection)
Dios no está enojado contigo (God Is Not Mad at You)
La dosis de aprobación (The Approval Fix)
Efesios: Comentario biblico (Ephesians: Biblical Commentary)
Empezando tu día bien (Starting Your Day Right)
Hágalo con miedo (Do It Afraid)
Hazte un favor a ti mismo…perdona (Do Yourself a Favor…Forgive)
Madre segura de sí misma (The Confident Mom)
Momentos de quietud con Dios (Quiet Times with God Devotional)
Mujer segura de sí misma (The Confident Woman)
No se afane por nada (Be Anxious for Nothing)
Pensamientos de poder (Power Thoughts)
Sanidad para el alma de una mujer (Healing the Soul of a Woman)
Sanidad para el alma de una mujer, devocionario (Healing the
Soul of a Woman Devotional)
Santiago: Comentario bíblico (James: Biblical Commentary)
Sobrecarga (Overload)*
Sus batallas son del Señor (Your Battles Belong to the Lord)
Termina bien tu día (Ending Your Day Right)
Tienes que atreverte (I Dare You)
Usted puede comenzar de nuevo (You Can Begin Again)
Viva amando su vida (Living a Life You Love)
Viva valientemente (Living Courageously)
Vive por encima de tus sentimientos (Living beyond Your Feelings)

* Study Guide available for this title

BOOKS BY DAVE MEYER

Life Lines